༄༅། མཁས་པའི་ཚུལ་ལ་འཇུག་པའི་སྒོ་ཞེས་བྱ་བའི་བསྟན་བཅོས་བཞུགས་སོ།།

mkhas pa'i tshul la jug pa'i sgo zhes bya ba'i bstan bcos bzhugs so.

Gateway to Knowledge

Vol. I

RANGJUNG YESHE BOOKS • *www.rangjung.com*

PADMASAMBHAVA • *Treasures from Juniper Ridge • Advice from the Lotus-Born, Dakini Teachings*

PADMASAMBHAVA AND JAMGÖN KONGTRÜL • *The Light of Wisdom, Vol. 1, & Vol. 2, Vol. 3, Secret, Vol. 4 & Vol. 5*

PADMASAMBHAVA, CHOKGYUR LINGPA, JAMYANG KHYENTSE WANGPO, TULKU URGYEN RINPOCHE, ORGYEN TOBGYAL RINPOCHE, & OTHERS • *Dispeller of Obstacles • The Tara Compendium • Powerful Transformation • Dakini Activity*

YESHE TSOGYAL • *The Lotus-Born*

DAKPO TASHI NAMGYAL • *Clarifying the Natural State*

TSELE NATSOK RANGDRÖL • *Mirror of Mindfulness • Heart Lamp*

CHOKGYUR LINGPA • *Ocean of Amrita • The Great Gate • Skillful Grace • Great Accomplishment • Guru Heart Practices*

TRAKTUNG DUDJOM LINGPA • *A Clear Mirror*

JAMGÖN MIPHAM RINPOCHE • *Gateway to Knowledge, Vol. 1, Vol. 2, Vol. 3, & Vol. 4*

TULKU URGYEN RINPOCHE • *Blazing Splendor • Rainbow Painting • As It Is, Vol. 1 • & Vol. 2 • Vajra Speech • Repeating the Words of the Buddha • Dzogchen Deity Practice*

ADEU RINPOCHE • *Freedom in Bondage*

KHENCHEN THRANGU RINPOCHE • *King of Samadhi • Crystal Clear*

CHÖKYI NYIMA RINPOCHE • *Present Fresh Wakefulness • Bardo Guidebook*

TULKU THONDUP • *Enlightened Living*

ORGYEN TOBGYAL RINPOCHE • *Life & Teachings of Chokgyur Lingpa*

DZIGAR KONGTRÜL RINPOCHE • *Uncommon Happiness*

TSOKNYI RINPOCHE • *Fearless Simplicity • Carefree Dignity*

MARCIA BINDER SCHMIDT • *Dzogchen Primer • Dzogchen Essentials • Quintessential Dzogchen • Confessions of a Gypsy Yogini • Precious Songs of Awakening Compilation*

ERIK PEMA KUNSANG • *Wellsprings of the Great Perfection • A Tibetan Buddhist Companion • The Rangjung Yeshe Tibetan-English Dictionary of Buddhist Culture & Perfect Clarity*

Gateway to Knowledge

The treatise entitled
The Gate for Entering the Way of a Pandita
by

Jamgön Mipham Rinpoche

Foreword by
CHÖKYI NYIMA RINPOCHE
Translated from the Tibetan by
ERIK PEMA KUNSANG

RANGJUNG YESHE PUBLICATIONS
Hong Kong, Boudhanath & Esby
1997

Rangjung Yeshe Publications
125 Robinson Road, flat 6a
Hong Kong

Address letters to:

Rangjung Yeshe Publications
P.O. Box 395
Leggett, CA 95585

1 3 5 7 9 8 6 4 2

First edition 1984
Second edition 1997
Third Edition 2008
Fourth Edition 2013

Special discount is given for classroom use. Write to the above address.

Distributed to the book trade by Perseus Books/Ingram

Printed in the United States of America

Publication Data:

Jamgön Mipham Rinpoche (Mi pham 'Jam dbyangs rNam rgyal rGya mtsho 1846–1912). Translated from the Tibetan by Erik Pema Kunsang (Erik Hein Schmidt). Edited by Marcia Binder Schmidt, with Kerry Moran.
1st edition.

Title: Gateway to Knowledge, The treatise entitled The Gate for Entering the Way of a Pandita.
Tibetan title: mkhas pa'i tshul la jug pa'i sgo zhes bya ba'i bstan bcos bzhugs so.

ISBN 978–962–7341–29–1 (pbk.)

1. Gateway to Knowledge; Vol. I. 2. Eastern philosophy — Buddhism.
3. Abhidharma — Tibet. I. Title.

The Tibetan is typeset in Sambhota font by Ugyen Shenphen and Gerry Wiener.

Table of Contents

Contents of the following volumes:

FOREWORD

Our teacher Buddha Shakyamuni is known as the Fourth Guide. He is the great loving kinsman of all sentient beings, who works for their welfare without being requested. Endowed with perfect wisdom, love, and ability, this truly and completely awakened one turned for us, his disciples, the profound and extensive Dharma Wheels. These teachings are the source for both temporary and ultimate happiness and well-being. In brief Buddha Shakyamuni presented the three vehicles. All that he gave is in harmony with how things are, with factual reasoning.

Especially in these times when the five degenerations are rampant, we need the very heart of the Buddha's teachings — loving kindness, compassion, and the knowledge that realizes egolessness. We are not only in need of his words; we need their meaning. However, merely byt hearing the words we still derive some benefit in that we feel joy and inspiration. There are numerous such reasons why the Buddha's teachings are spreading all over the world and gaining popularity in various countries, among many different races of people.

The Buddha's words are both profound and extensive, and to understand them fully we use the three stages of knowledge that result from learning, from reflection and from training.

The knowledge that results from learning is the understanding we gain when studying with a true master. We do this by listening to explanations from a qualified spiritual teacher of what the Buddha taught and the commentaries that clarify his teachings. Reading through the Buddha's sublime words and treatises also is included under learning.

The knowledge from reflection is the understanding we arrive at through our personal questioning and examination of the meaning. We can check for ourselves whether or not a statement agrees with factual logic. We can question what the immediate benefit and the ultimate result of training is and how we can personally apply it. By thoroughly scrutinizing the reason and purpose we gain a certain comprehension that is called the knowledge that results from reflection.

These two — learning and reflection — give us an intellectual understanding. The process of assimilating this within our experience brings another type of understanding known as the knowledge resulting from training. This personalized knowledge, when recognized and stabilized, is the source for the same realization reached by the Buddha. In the usual terminology it is called *sugata-garbha*, in the extraordinary teachings of Vajrayana we call it intrinsic wakefulness, self-existing awareness, the ultimate real condition. This is what we must recognize.

Through recognizing this real condition in an authentic way, we can, within a very short time, gather the accumulations and purify the obscurations. Moreover we can reduce all our disturbing emotions, naturally and automatically. In this way we are able to experience the original wakefulness that is realization. In short, by following this path we remove very quickly all shortcomings and manifest all qualities, effortlessly and spontaneously.

This is possible because the basis for realization, the very essence of what the Buddha taught, is within ourselves. The buddha is within; all the qualities of enlightenment are present within our own nature. This is the principal point in which we must exert ourselves, in which we must train.

Our real condition, our natural state, is most precious and wonderful. To gain an intimate knowledge of this for ourselves and to make it known to others is why we must study the Buddha's sublime teachings and the treatises that clarify them.

This need for learning provides the context in which we now present the treatise entitled *The Gate for Entering the Way of a Pandita.* Jamgön Mipham Rinpoche (1846-1912), was likewise known as Ju Mipham, (his family name was Ju), Mipham Jampal Yang, or as Mipham Jamyang Namgyal Gyamtso. He studied with many great masters from all traditions. Furthermore he received teachings on the traditional topics of knowledge as well as a vast number of empowerments, transmissions, and instructions. Gifted with a natural intelligence, Jamgön Mipham Rinpoche became extremely learned. He was accomplished in all five fields of knowledge and remains the example of perfect scholarship. When we reflect on him as a practitioner, it seems that he spent his entire life in retreat. If we contemplate his writings, it seems that he spent his entire life composing treatises. If we consider his work as a Dharma teacher, it seems that he spent his entire life giving teachings. By reading his life story we can ascertain that his accomplishments are incredible. In short, how he studied, reflected, practiced; how he taught, discussed and composed; his deeds in learning and teaching the treatises are immense and unprejudiced.

Among the extensive literature he authored, *The Gateway to Knowledge*, has a vital importance for followers of Buddhism. Why is that? It is not because it is vast and detailed; because it isn't. However by studying this text and learning it well, you ensure that you have gained a rough comprehension of what the Buddha taught in general. In particular *The Gateway to Knowledge* will form the circumstance for more easily understanding all the sublime words and treatises, such as the works of Nagarjuna. It is for these many reasons that Ju Mipham's *Gateway to Knowledge* is extremely important.

What are the substance and contents of *The Gateway to Knowledge*? As I just mentioned, it functions as a key for gaining a preliminary understanding of the sublime words and the treatises. Specifically the student of this text can begin to comprehend the meaning of the major works on Buddhist philosophy and of the traditional sciences to a lesser degree.

The sublime words and the treatises of the Sutra and Tantra systems are a very vast and profound topic to study. When you want to extract this meaning you need an "expert system," a key. *The Gateway to Knowledge* is like that key, a magical key — it opens up the treasury of precious gemstones in the expansive collection of Buddhist scriptures.

Once you have scrutinized *The Gateway to Knowledge*, those of you who wish to proceed to the major works of Buddhist philosophy will find it quite easy to understand them. *The Gateway to Knowledge* is in itself an excellent Buddhist study text. In particular, it is helpful for your further studies.

Over the years, for these and many other reasons, I have insistently and repeatedly asked Erik Pema Kunsang to translate this work. Since he has both affection and respect for me, he took my request seriously and undertook many difficulties to do so. The result is shown is this publication, the first volume, and in the volumes to come.

You, the readers, please study it carefully, and take the meaning to heart. May this be a flawless cause for you to uphold the precious teachings of the Buddha through correct learning, reflection and meditation training. May it benefit you individually and assist you in benefiting others through teaching, composition, and discussion. This is my intention, my hope, and my aspiration. Tashi Delek.

—Chökyi Nyima Rinpoche

Acknowledgments

Teachers consulted for transmission and clarifications:

Khenchen Thrangu Rinpoche
Chökyi Nyima Rinpoche
Khenpo Tsültrim Gyatso Rinpoche
Dzogchen Ponlop Rinpoche
Khenpo Ngedön
Khenpo Chökyi Gocha
Khenpo Könchok Mönlam
Khenpo Chödrak Tenpel

Assistant translators and editors:
Marcia Binder Schmidt, Kerry Moran and Judith Amtzis

The present translation is thanks to Chökyi Nyima Rinpoche's constant guidance, encouragement and prodding; to the compassion and wisdom of the teachers mentioned above; to the generous sponsorship of George MacDonald; and to the kindness of all my Dharma friends who helped at various stages of this project. Special thanks to Scott Wellenbach for providing notes from Ponlop Rinpoche's teachings on the first chapter.

Since this edition is meant for classroom use, we decided to include the original Tibetan text. To help the readers, the words within square brackets that have been included are from *Lekshey Nangwey Özer*, the *chendrel* (filling-in) commentary written down by Mipham Rinpoche's student Khenpo Nüden. This commentary, which incorporates the oral explanations of Shechen Gyaltsab Pema Namgyal, was also consulted to supply the end notes.

Lastly, we would like to express our gratitude to Kyabje Dilgo Khyentse Rinpoche, who in the early days after leaving Tibet, personally sponsored the woodblocks that were the source of our Tibetan manuscript.

༄༅། མཁས་པའི་ཚུལ་ལ་འཇུག་པའི་སྒོ་ཞེས་བྱ་བའི་བསྟན་བཅོས་བཞུགས་སོ།།

mkhas pa'i tshul la jug pa'i sgo zhes bya ba'i bstan bcos bzhugs so.

Gateway to Knowledge

༄༅། མཁས་པའི་ཚུལ་ལ་འཇུག་པའི་སྒོ་ཞེས་བྱ་བའི་བསྟན་བཅོས་བཞུགས་སོ།

རྒྱ་གར་སྐད་དུ། པཎྜིཏ་སྦུ་ན་ཡོ་ཨ་ཕ་ཏཱ་ར་སུ་ཁཿ་ནཱ་མ་ཤཱསྟྲ།

བོད་སྐད་དུ། མཁས་པའི་ཚུལ་ལ་འཇུག་པའི་སྒོ་ཞེས་བྱ་བའི་བསྟན་བཅོས།

དཀོན་མཆོག་གསུམ་ལ་ཕྱག་འཚལ་ལོ།

།དོན་བཅུ་ཡང་དག་ཐུགས་སུ་ཆུད་གྱུར་ཅིང་། ཕྱག་རྒྱ་བཞི་ཡི་དོན་ནི་འགྲོ་ལ་སྟོན། ཚིག་དོན་དྲི་མེད་ཆོས་རབ་སྣང་བའི་གཏེར། སྨྲ་བའི་ཉི་མ་སྙིང་ལ་འཇུག་པར་མཛོད།

།འདིར་ཤེས་བྱའི་གནས་མ་ནོར་བར་གཏན་ལ་འབེབས་པའི་ཤེས་རབ་འཐོབ་པར་འདོད་པས་མདོ་དང་བསྟན་བཅོས་ཆེན་པོ་རྣམས་ལས་གསུངས་པ་ལྟར་མཁས་པར་བྱ་བའི་གནས་བཅུ་ལ་བསླབ་པར་བྱ་སྟེ། གང་ཞེ་ན་ཕུང་པོ་ལ་མཁས་པ་དང་། དེ་བཞིན་དུ་ཁམས་དང་སྐྱེ་མཆེད་དང་། རྟེན་འབྲེལ་དང་། གནས་དང་གནས་མ་ཡིན་པ་དང་། དབང་པོ་དང་། དུས་དང་། བདེན་པ་དང་། ཐེག་པ་དང་། འདུས་བྱས་འདུས་མ་བྱས་ལ་མཁས་པ་དང་བཅུའོ།

Prologue

Sanskrit title: Pandita Syanayam Avataramukha Nama Shastrasti.

Tibetan title: mkhas pa'i tshul la jug pa'i sgo zhes bya ba'i bstan bcos bzhugs so.

English title: The treatise entitled The Gate for Entering the Way of a Pandita.

Homage to the Three Jewels.

Comprehending perfectly the ten topics,[1]
You teach beings the meaning of the Four Seals.[2]
Treasure who fully illuminates the teachings of flawless word
and meaning,[3]
Sun of Speech, may you enter our hearts.[4]

If you desire to attain the discriminating knowledge that unmistakenly ascertains what should be known, you should study these ten topics which cause learnedness, as is taught in the great sutras and treatises. What are they? They are the ten topics of being learned in: 1) the aggregates; 2) the elements; 3) the sources; 4) dependent origination; 5) the correct and the incorrect; 6) the faculties; 7) time; 8) the truths; 9) the vehicles; 10) conditioned things and unconditioned things.

By the power of gaining certainty in these ten topics, you will be freed from the delusions of unwholesome views that should be

།འདི་བཅུ་གཏན་ལ་ཕབ་པའི་ཤུགས་ཀྱིས་སྤྱང་བྲུ་བདག་ཏུ་ལྟ་བ་བཅུ་ལྡོག་པ་སོགས་ལྟ་བ་ངན་པའི་རྨོངས་པ་ཀུན་ལས་གྲོལ་ཞིང་། ཇི་ལྟ་ཇི་སྙེད་ཀྱི་བློ་གྲོས་རྒྱས་པར་འགྱུར་བ་ཡིན་ནོ།

abandoned, such as banishing the ten types of self-oriented views and so forth, and you will increase the wisdom of things as they are and of all that exists.

།ཕུང་པོ་ནི་ལྔ་སྟེ། གཟུགས་ཀྱི་ཕུང་པོ་དང༌། ཚོར་བའི་ཕུང་པོ་དང༌། འདུ་ཤེས་ཀྱི་ཕུང་པོ་དང༌། འདུ་བྱེད་ཀྱི་ཕུང་པོ་དང༌། རྣམ་པར་ཤེས་པའི་ཕུང་པོའོ།

།གཟུགས་གང་ཅི་ཡང་རུང་བ་དུས་གསུམ་དང༌། ཕྱི་ནང་སོགས་དང༌། རྣམ་པ་བཟང་ངན་སོགས་ཐམས་ཅད་བསྡུས་ཏེ་གཟུགས་ཀྱི་ཕུང་པོར་བཞག་པ་དེ་བཞིན་ཚོར་བ་སོགས་ལའང་ཤེས་པར་བྱ་སྟེ། དུ་མ་སྤུངས་པས་ན་ཕུང་པོ་ཞེས་བྱའོ།

།དེ་ལ་གཟུགས་སུ་རུང་བའི་མཚན་ཉིད་ཅན་གྱི་ཕུང་པོ་དེ་ལ་དབྱེ་ན། རྒྱུ་གཟུགས་བཞི། འབྲས་གཟུགས་བཅུ་གཅིག་གོ།

རྒྱུ་ནི་འབྱུང་བ་ཆེན་པོ་བཞི་སྟེ། སའི་ཁམས་ནི་སྲ་ཞིང་གཞི་འཛིན་པའི་ལས་བྱེད་པ། ཆུ་ཁམས་གཤེར་ཞིང་སྡུད་པ། མེ་ཁམས་དྲོ་ཞིང་སྨིན་པ། རླུང་ཁམས་གཡོ་ཞིང་འཕེལ་བར་བྱེད་པའོ།

1
The Aggregates
Skandha

[1,1] There are five aggregates: the aggregate of forms, the aggregate of sensations, the aggregate of perceptions, the aggregates of formations, and the aggregate of consciousnesses.

[1,2] All possible forms, in whichever of the three times, in a near or distant place, or of a good or bad type, are, when grouped together, defined as the aggregate of forms. It should here be understood that the same applies to [the aggregates of] sensations, [perceptions] and so forth. Thus, aggregate is so called because of being an aggregation of many parts.

The Aggregate of Forms

[1,3] The aggregate of what is defined as [physical] forms can be subdivided into the four causal forms and the eleven resultant forms.

[1,4] Causal [forms] are the four primary elements. The earth element is solidity and its function is to support. The water element is fluidity and cohesion. The fire element is heat and ripening. The wind element is motion and expansion.

།འབྲས་གཟུགས་བཅུ་གཅིག་ནི། དབང་པོ་ལྔ་དང༌། དོན་ལྔ་དང་བཅུ། མཚོན་ལྟར་ན་རྣམ་པར་རིག་བྱེད་མིན་པའི་གཟུགས་དང་བཅུ་གཅིག། ཀུན་བཏུས་ལྟར་ན་ཆོས་ཀྱི་སྐྱེ་མཆེད་པའི་གཟུགས་དང་བཅུ་གཅིག་གོ།

།གཟུགས་ཕུང་འདི་དག་རེག་པ་དང་དཔྱད་པའི་སྒོ་ནས་གཟུགས་སུ་ཡོད་པར་བཞག་སྟེ། དང་པོ་ལག་པ་དང་དབྱུག་པ་དང་རླུང་སོགས་ཀྱིས་ཐུག་རེག་ཡོད་པ་དང༌། གཉིས་པ་མཉམ་པར་བཞག་པའམ་མ་བཞག་པའི་ཡིད་རྟོག་བཅས་ཀྱིས་གཟུགས་འདི་ནི་འདི་ལྟ་བུའོ། །ཞེས་བཀྲ་བར་བཟུང་བས་སོ།

།དེ་ལ་དབང་པོ་ལྔ་ནི། མིག་གི་དབང་པོ་དང༌། དེ་བཞིན་དུ་རྣ་བ་སྣ་ལྕེ་ལུས་ཀྱི་དབང་པོའོ། །དབང་པོ་ལྔ་པོ་འདི་དག་རང་རང་གི་ཤེས་པའི་བདག་རྐྱེན་ཐུན་མོང་མིན་པ་ནང་གི་གཟུགས་ཅན་དྭང་བ་སྟེ།

མིག་གི་དབང་པོ་ཟར་མའི་མེ་ཏོག་ལྟ་བུ། རྣ་བའི་དབང་པོ་གྲོ་གའི་འཛེར་བུ་གཙུས་པ་ལྟ་བུ། སྣའི་དབང་པོ་ཟངས་ཀྱི་མོ་ཁབ་གཤིབས་པ་ལྟ་བུ། ལྕེའི་དབང་པོ་ཟླ་བ་བཀས་པ་ལྟ་བུ། ལུས་ཀྱི་དབང་པོ་བྱ་རེག་ན་འཇམ་གྱི་པགས་པ་ལྟ་བུའོ།

།དོན་ལྔ་ནི། གཟུགས་སྒྲ་དྲི་རོ་རེག་བྱའོ།

།གཟུགས་ནི་མིག་གི་ཡུལ་ཏེ། དེ་ལ་དབྱེ་ན་ཁ་དོག་དང༌། དབྱིབས་ཀྱི་གཟུགས་གཉིས། དང་པོ་ལ་སྔོ་སེར་དཀར་དམར་རྩ་བའི་ཁ་དོག་བཞི། དེའི་ཡན་ལག་ཏུ། སྤྲིན་དང་དུ་བ། རྡུལ་དང་ཁུག་སྣ། ཉི་འོད་གྲིབ་མ། སྣང་བ་མུན་པ་རྣམས་དང༌།

[1,5] The eleven resultant forms are the five sense faculties and the five sense objects, together totaling ten. According to the *Abhidharma Kosha* the eleventh type is imperceptible forms. According to the *Abhidharma Samucchaya* the eleventh type is the forms that are mental objects.

[1,6] These form aggregates are defined as having form by means of contact or inference. The first case refers to the fact they can be touched by a hand, a stick, the wind or by other things. The second case [of inference] implies a certain form can be clearly perceived as being such-and-such by either the composed [meditative] frame of mind, or by the conceptual frame of mind not composed in meditation.

[1,7] The five sense faculties are the eye faculty and likewise the ear, nose, tongue, and body faculties. The five faculties are the particular ruling factors for their respective cognitions. They are inner subtle forms [based on the physical sense organ].

[1,8] The [shape of the] eye faculty is similar to [the round and blue shape of] the *umaka* [sesame/cumin] flower; the ear faculty is similar to [the shape of] a twisted roll of birch bark; the nose faculty is similar to [the shape of] parallel copper needles; the tongue faculty is similar to [the shape of] a crescent moon disc; and the body faculty is [all-covering] similar to the skin of the smooth-to-the-touch bird.

[1,9] The five sense objects are visible forms, sounds, odors, tastes, and textures.

[1,10] Visible forms are the sense objects of the eye. They can be divided into two types: color-forms and shape-forms.

[1,11] Concerning the first [color-form], the four primary colors are blue, yellow, white, and red. The secondary colors are cloudy and smoky, dusty and misty, sunny and shady, light and dark.

ཡང་མངོན་པར་སྐབས་ཡོད་པ་ཞེས་པ་གཟུགས་དེ་གཞན་ལ་ཐོགས་པར་བྱེད་པའི་རེག་བྱ་དང་བྲལ་བ་བར་སྣང་སྐྱ་སེང་པོ་ལྟ་བུ་གཟུགས་བརྙན་སོགས་ཀྱང་དེ་དང་ཆ་འདྲའོ།

།ཕྱག་འཚལ་བ་ལྟ་བུ་སོགས་རྣམ་པ་རིག་བྱེད། སྙིང་གི་ནམ་མཁའ་སྔོན་པོ་ཁ་དོག་གཅིག་པ་རྣམས་ཏེ་འདི་རྣམས་ཀྱང་གཟུགས་སུ་བསྡུ་བའི་ཆེད་དུ་བཀོད་དོ།

།རྩ་བའི་ཁ་དོག་གི་ཆ་ཤས་འདྲེས་པ་ལས་བྱེ་བྲག་གི་ཡན་ལག་མང་དུ་འགྱུར་རོ།

།དབྱིབས་གཟུགས་ལ། རིང་པོ། ཐུང་ངུ། ལྷམ་པ། ཟླུམ་པོ། མཐོ་བ། དམའ་བ། ཕྲ་བ། རགས་པ། ཕྱལ་ལེ་བ། ཕྱལ་ལེ་བ་མ་ཡིན་པ་རྣམས་ཀྱིས་སྤྱིར་བསྟན་ཏེ། ནང་གི་དབྱེ་བ་ལ། གྲུ་གསུམ། ཟླ་གམ། འཇོང་མོ་སོགས་མང་པོར་འགྱུར་རོ།

།དབྱིབས་དང་ཁ་དོག་དེ་དག་བཟང་ངན་བར་མ་གསུམ་དུ་འདུའོ།

།སྒྲ་ནི་རྣ་བའི་ཡུལ་ཏེ། དེ་ལ་ཟིན་པའི་འབྱུང་བའི་རྒྱུ་ལས་བྱུང་བ་སེམས་ཅན་གྱི་ངག་དང་སེ་གོལ་གྱི་སྒྲ་ལྟ་བུ། མ་ཟིན་པའི་འབྱུང་བའི་རྒྱུ་ལས་བྱུང་བ། ཆུ་ཀླུང་དང་རླུང་སོགས་ཀྱི་སྒྲ་ལྟ་བུ། གཉིས་ཀ་ལས་བྱུང་བ་རྔ་བརྡུང་བའི་སྒྲ་ལྟ་བུ། སེམས་ཅན་དུ་སྟོན་པ་དོན་རྗོད་པར་བྱེད་པ། སེམས་ཅན་དུ་མི་སྟོན་པ་དོན་རྗོད་པར་མི་བྱེད་པ། དོན་རྗོད་བྱེད་ལ་འཇིག་རྟེན་པས་ཐ་སྙད་བཏགས་པ། འཕགས་པས་ཐ་སྙད་བཏགས་པ་སོགས་ཀྱི་ཁྱད་པར་ཡོད་ཅིང་།

དེ་དག་ལ་སྙན་མི་སྙན་བར་མའི་དབྱེ་བ་རྣམས་སོ།

།དྲི་ནི་སྣའི་ཡུལ་ཏེ། དེ་ལ་དྲི་ཞིམ་མི་ཞིམ། ཆ་མཉམ་པ། ལྷན་སྐྱེས། སྦྱོར་བྱུང་ངོ།

།རོ་ནི་ལྕེའི་ཡུལ་ཏེ། མངར་བ། སྐྱུར་བ། ལན་ཚྭ་བ། ཁ་བ། ཚ་བ། བསྐ་བ་དྲུག་དང་། དེ་དག་འདྲེས་པ་ལས་ནང་གི་དབྱེ་བ་དུ་མར་གྱུར་རོ། ཡང་ཡིད་དུ་འོང་མི་འོང་བར་མ་གསུམ་དང་།

Spatial [form] is a visible form, for example, pure, clear space, free from something tangible that impedes other things. Reflections and so forth belong to this type.

Perceptible [forms] such as the act of prostrating and the uniformly colored blue sky are also said to be included under visible forms.

Many different secondary colors come about by mixing the primary colors.

[1,12] Shape-forms are, in general, said to be long or short, square or round, concave or convex, fine or gross, even or uneven. There are many subdivisions such as triangular, crescent-shaped, oblong, and so forth.

These shapes and colors can be classed as attractive, repulsive, or neutral.

[1,13] Sounds are the sense objects of the ear. There are different kinds: sounds that originate from conscious elemental causes such as the voice of a sentient being or a finger snap; sounds that originate from unconscious elemental causes such as the sounds of a river, the wind and so forth; sounds that originate from both [conscious and unconscious elements] such as a drum beat; animate sounds that express meaning; and inanimate sounds that don't express meaning. Sounds that express meaning can be either spoken by a mundane person or by a noble person.

Sounds can also be divided into pleasant, unpleasant and neutral.

[1,14] Odors are the sense objects of the nose. There are odors that are fragrant, non-fragrant, or neutral, and those that are natural or manufactured.

[1,15] Tastes are the sense objects of the tongue. There are six kinds: sweet, sour, salty, bitter, pungent, and astringent. Many subsidiary types come about from mixing them. Tastes also have the divisions of being pleasant, unpleasant, or neutral, as well as being natural or manufactured.

ལྡན་སྐྱེས་དང་། སྦྱར་བྱུང་གི་དབྱེ་བ་ཡང་ཡོད་དོ།

།རིག་བྱ་ནི་ལུས་ཀྱི་ཡུལ་ཏེ། རྒྱུ་འབྱུང་བ་བཞིའི་རིག་བྱ་དང་། འབྲས་བུ་ལ། འཇམ་རྩུབ་ལྕི་ཡང་བཀྲེས་སྐོམ་གྲང་བ་བདུན་དང་། མཉེན་པ། ལྷོད་པ། དམ་པ། ཚིམ་པ། ན་བ། རྒ་བ། འཆི་བ། ངལ་སོས་པ། སྤྲངས་ཆེ་བ་ཞེས་མི་འཇིགས་པ་སྟེ་ལུས་སྟོབས་དང་ལྡན་ནས་མ་ཞུམ་པའོ། འདི་དག་གིས་མཚོན་ནས་ལུས་ཀྱི་ཕྱི་དང་ནང་གི་རིག་བྱ་སྐྱོང་ཚུལ་དུ་མ་ཡོད་པ་ཤེས་པར་བྱའོ།

།ཆོས་ཀྱི་སྐྱེ་མཆེད་པའི་གཟུགས་ལྔ་སྟེ།

བསྡུས་པ་ལས་གྱུར་པ་ཞེས་པ་རྡུལ་ཕྲ་རབ་ཀྱི་གཟུགས་ནི་གཟུགས་ཡིན་ཀྱང་ཡིད་ཀྱིས་ཤེས་པར་བྱ་བ་ཙམ་མོ།

།མངོན་པར་སྐབས་ཡོད་པའམ་གསལ་བ་ནི་གོང་བཤད་ལྟར་གཞན་ལ་མི་ཐོགས་པའོ།

།ཡང་དག་པར་བླངས་པ་ལས་བྱུང་བ་ནི་རྣམ་པར་རིག་བྱེད་མ་ཡིན་པའི་གཟུགས་སོ།

།ཀུན་བརྟགས་པའི་གཟུགས་ནི་གཟུགས་བརྙན་དང་རྨི་ལམ་གྱི་གཟུགས་ལྟ་བུའོ།

།དབང་འབྱོར་བའི་གཟུགས་ནི་བསམ་གཏན་ལ་དབང་འབྱོར་བའི་སྟོབས་ཀྱིས་སྣང་བའི་གཟུགས་ཟད་པར་སྔོན་པོ་ལ་སོགས་པ་ལྟ་བུའོ།

།དབང་འབྱོར་བའི་གཟུགས་ལྟ་བུ་སེམས་པོ་ནའི་སྟོབས་ཀྱིས་སྣང་བ་ལ་ནི་རྡུལ་ཕྲན་བསགས་པ་མེད་པའི་ཕྱིར་དེའི་རྒྱུ་འབྱུང་བ་རྣམས་མ་ཡིན་ཏེ་དེ་ལས་གཞན་པའི་གཟུགས་ཀྱི་དབང་དུ་མཛད་ནས་དེ་ལྟར་རྒྱུར་གསུངས་སོ།

།རྣམ་པར་རིག་བྱེད་མིན་པ་འདི་གཟུགས་ཇི་ལྟར་ཡིན་ཅེ་ན།

[1,16] Textures are the sense objects of the body. There are the textures of the four causal forms[7] and the seven [textures of] the resultant ones, which are smoothness, roughness, heaviness, lightness, and [the inner physical sensations of] hunger, thirst and cold. There are also the textures of being supple, yielding or rigid, and [the inner physical sensations of feeling] sated, ill, aged, dying, rested, and bold. Bold means feeling fearless, not shying away due to [one's own] bodily strength.

As indicated by these, please understand that there are numerous ways of experiencing external and internal bodily textures.

[1,17] There are five types of forms that are mental objects:

1) Deduced forms are the forms of the smallest particles, which, although physical, can only be known mentally.

2) Spatial forms or clear forms are forms that cannot impede other things, as explained above.

3) Forms resulting from a taken promise are imperceptible forms.[8]

4) Imagined forms are such things as a [mental] image or dreamt forms.

5) Mastered forms are forms appearing through the power of mastery in meditation, such as the totality of blue.

[1,18] Mastered forms, it is taught, appear solely due to the power of mind and are not a conglomeration of particles. Their substance is therefore not the elements but is said to be substance in the sense of a physical form different from them [from the four elements].

[1,19] How can something imperceptible be a physical form? Imperceptible form is defined as physical form because of these [three] reasons.

1. Imperceptible form is an action of body or speech after having obtained a [virtuous] vow, a unvirtuous vow, or a vow with limited time span. It does, however, not consist of cognition because

འདི་ནི་སྡོམ་སྡོམ་མིན་བར་སྡོམ་ཐོབ་པའི་ལུས་ངག་གི་ལས་ཞིག་ཡིན་ལ། དེ་ནི་གཡེང་བ་དང་སེམས་མེད་པའི་སྐབས་སུའང་རྒྱུན་མ་ཆད་པར་ཡོད་པས་སེམས་ཀྱིས་བསྡུས་པ་མིན་པ་དང་། དང་པོར་རང་རྒྱུད་ཀྱི་ཟིན་པའི་འབྱུང་བ་རྣམས་རྒྱུར་བྱས་ནས་སྐྱེ་ཞིང་། ཟིན་འབྱུང་དེ་ལ་བརྟེན་ཏེ་ཇི་སྲིད་རྟེན་ཉམས་པའམ་གཏོང་རྒྱུ་མ་བྱུང་གི་བར་དུ་རྒྱུན་ཆགས་པར་འབྱུང་བ་ཡིན་པ་དང་། ངོ་བོ་དགེ་མི་དགེ་གང་རུང་དུ་ངེས་པ་ལུས་ངག་གི་ལས་ཀྱི་བྱེ་བྲག་ཞིག་ཡིན་པའི་རྒྱུ་མཚན་གསུམ་པོ་དེས་གཟུགས་སུ་འཛོག་པ་ཡིན་ནོ།

།དེ་ཡང་དད་པས་ཕྱག་འཚལ་བའམ། མདོ་འདོན་པ་དང་སྡང་བས་གཞན་ལ་བརྡེག་པ་དང་ཚིག་རྩུབ་སྨྲ་བ་ལྟ་བུའི་ལས་ནི། རྒྱུ་ལུས་ངག་གི་རྡུལ་རྣམས་ལས་ཡན་གར་དུ་མེད་ཀྱང་། ལུས་ངག་གཡོ་བ་དང་བཀོད་པའི་རྣམ་འགྱུར་ཁྱད་པར་བ་དེ་ལ་ལས་སུ་འཛོག་དགོས་སོ།

།ལས་དེས་ནི་རང་ཀུན་ནས་སློང་བྱེད་ལུས་ངག་གི་རྡུལ་གྱི་ཚོགས་པ་རྣམས་གཞན་ལ་རིག་པར་བྱེད་དེ། ཇི་ལྟར་ན་རྡེའུ་དུ་མ་ཏ་སོགས་ཀྱི་དབྱིབས་སུ་བཀོད་པ་མཐོང་བ་ན། རྡེའུ་རྣམས་མཐོང་བ་ཡིན་གྱི་དེ་ལས་གཞན་མཐོང་རྒྱུ་ཅི་ཡང་མེད་མོད། རྡེའུ་རྣམས་མཐོང་བའི་སྒོ་ནས་རྡེའུ་རྣམས་བཀོད་ལུགས་ཀྱི་དབྱིབས་དེ་ཡང་ཤེས་པ་བཞིན་ནོ།

།རིག་བྱེད་མིན་གཟུགས་ཀྱང་ལུས་ངག་གི་ལས་ཀྱི་ཁྱད་པར་ཡིན་པ་ལ་རིག་བྱེད་ཀྱི་གཟུགས་དང་འདྲ་ཡང་། དེས་རང་ཀུན་ནས་སློང་བྱེད་ལུས་ངག་གི་ཆ་དེ་རང་གི་རྒྱུ་ཡིན་པར་གཞན་ལ་རིག་པར་མི་བྱེད་དེ། སྡོམ་ལྡན་གྱི་གང་ཟག་གི་སྡོམ་པ་འདི་ལྟ་བུའོ་ཞེས་དེའི་ལུས་སོགས་མཐོང་བ་ཙམ་གྱིས་མི་ཤེས་པ་བཞིན་ནོ།

།དེས་ན་འདི་ལ་རྣམ་པར་རིག་བྱེད་མིན་པ་དང་། བསྟན་མེད་ཐོགས་མེད་ཀྱི་གཟུགས་ཞེས་བྱ་

it is continuously present even at times of distraction or the absence of cognizance.

2. Imperceptible form first arises from elements embraced by one's stream-of-being. Based on these embraced elements, it continues until its support degenerates or a cause for abandoning it occurs.

3. Imperceptible form is a certain kind of physical or verbal action. Its identity is determined as being either virtuous or unvirtuous.

For instance, the substance of the act of prostrating out of faith, chanting a sutra, beating others or speaking harshly out of anger, is nothing other than the material body and speech. It is, nonetheless, a particular physical movement or verbal expression and should therefore be defined as a [karmic] action.

By means of such an action, the gathering of physical or verbal particles activated by oneself is made perceptible to others. How is that? When seeing a number of pebbles arranged in the shape of a horse, for instance, one sees all the pebbles and there is indeed nothing else to see other than them. Yet, by means of seeing the pebbles one also understands the shape in which the pebbles are arranged.

[1,20] Imperceptible forms are also a particular feature of physical or verbal actions. Though similar to perceptible forms, through them alone it is not perceptible to others that the physical or verbal aspects [of an action] activated by oneself are one's own substance. For instance, a particular vow taken by a person is not [readily] perceived merely by seeing his body. [These kind of forms] are therefore called imperceptible forms, undemonstratable forms, or unobstructing forms.

[1,21] Because of being a conglomeration of particles, the ten faculties and objects are composites made of the ultimately smallest form, that is to say, gatherings of the most subtle and partless atoms.

བར་བརྗོད་དོ།

།དབང་དོན་བཅུ་པོ་དེ་དག་རྡུལ་ཕྲན་བསགས་པ་ཡིན་པའི་ཕྱིར་གཟུགས་ཀྱི་མཐའ་ཕྲ་རབ་ཆ་མེད་ཀྱི་རྡུལ་ལས་བརྩམས་ཏེ་ཇེ་རྒྱས་སུ་འགྱུར་ཏེ།

ཇི་ལྟར་ན་རྡུལ་ཕྲ་རབ་བདུན་ལ་རྡུལ་ཕྲན་གཅིག་ཅེས་བྱའོ། །དེ་བཞིན་བདུན་འགྱུར་གྱིས། ལྕགས་ཆུ་རི་བོང་ལུག་གླང་། ཉི་ཟེར་གྱི་རྡུལ་དང་། སྲོ་མ་དང་། ཤིག་དང་། ནས་དང་སོར་ཚིགས་ཀྱི་ཚད་ཀྱི་བར་དུའོ། །སོར་མོ་ཉེར་བཞི་ལ་ཁྲུ་གང་ངོ་། །ཁྲུ་བཞི་གཞུ་འདོམ་གང་ངོ་། །གཞུ་འདོམ་ལྔ་བརྒྱ་ལ་རྒྱང་གྲགས་ཀྱི་ཚད་ཅེས་བྱའོ། །རྒྱང་གྲགས་བརྒྱད་ལ་དཔག་ཚད་གཅིག་སྟེ། དཔག་ཚད་དེས་རི་གླིང་སོགས་ཀྱི་ཚད་འཇལ་བར་བྱེད་དོ།

།འདོད་ཁམས་ན་དབང་པོ་དང་སྒྲ་མེད་པའི་རྡུལ་གང་ལ་ཡང་འབྱུང་བཞི་དང་གཟུགས་དྲི་རོ་རེག་གི་རྡུལ་བརྒྱད་ཡོད་ལ། སྒྲ་ཡོད་ན་སྒྲ་རྡུལ་དང་དགུ། ལུས་དབང་ཡོད་ན་དེའི་རྡུལ་དང་བཅུ། དབང་པོ་གཞན་ཡོད་ན་ལུས་དབང་དེ་དང་ལྷན་ཅིག་ཡོད་པས་རྡུལ་རིགས་མི་འདྲ་བ་བཅུ་གཅིག་ཡོད་དོ།

།ཚོར་བ་ནི་ཉམས་སུ་མྱོང་བའི་མཚན་ཉིད་ཅན་ནོ།

།ཚོར་བའི་ཕུང་པོ་དེ་ལ་དབྱེ་ན། བདེ་སྡུག་བཏང་སྙོམས་གསུམ་མམ། བདེ་བ་ཡིད་བདེ། སྡུག་བསྔལ་ཡིད་མི་བདེ་གཉིས་སུ་ཕྱེས་ན་ཚོར་བ་བཏང་སྙོམས་དང་དེ་ལྔའོ།

།རྟེན་གྱི་དབང་དུ་བྱས་ན་མིག་རྣ་སྣ་ལྕེ་ལུས་ཡིད་ཀྱི་འདུས་ཏེ་རེག་པ་ལས་བྱུང་བའི་ཚོར་བ་དྲུག་དང་། དེ་ལ་བདེ་སྡུག་བཏང་སྙོམས་གསུམ་གྱི་དབྱེ་བས་ཡིད་ཉེ་བར་རྒྱུ་བའི་ཚོར་བ་བཅོ་བརྒྱད་དུ་འགྱུར་རོ།

[1,22] Seven most subtle atoms [joined together] are called one particle. Multiplying it by seven results in a measure called the iron particle. [Seven iron particles are one] water [particle, and so on upwards to] the rabbit [particle], the sheep [particle], the cow [particle], the sunbeam [particle], the [size of a] louse egg, a louse, a barley grain, and a finger width. Twenty-four finger widths are one cubit. Four cubits are one fathom. Five hundred fathoms are one mile, and eight miles are one league. The size of Mount Sumeru and the continents is measured in leagues.

[1,23] In the Desire Realms the eight types of particles consisting of the four [primary] elements and [the four properties] of form, odor, taste, and textures are always present. The particles of the sense faculties and of sound are not counted [because they are not always present]. When a sound is present, then the presence of the sound particle makes nine. If the body is present, then the presence of the particle of its [faculty] makes ten [particles]. If any of the other faculties are present, then there are eleven different types of particles due to that [faculty] being coexistent with the body faculty.

Sensations

[1,24] Sensations are defined as impressions.

[1,25] The aggregate of sensations can be divided into three: pleasant, painful, and neutral. Alternately, there are five: pleasure and mental pleasure, pain and mental pain, and neutral sensation.

[1,26] In terms of the support, there are the six sensations resulting from contact, involving the meeting of [sense object, faculty and consciousness of] either eye, ear, nose, tongue, body, or mind. When divided [dividing those six in terms of pleasure, pain, and indifference], there are eighteen types of sensation accompanying a cognitive act.

།གཞན་ཡང་སྒོ་ལྔའི་ཤེས་པ་དང་མཚུངས་ལྡན་ལུས་ཚོར། ཡིད་ཤེས་དང་མཚུངས་ལྡན་སེམས་ཚོར། ལུས་ལ་སྲིད་པ་དང་མཚུངས་ལྡན་གྱི་ཚོར་བ་ཟང་ཟིང་བཅས་པ། སྲིད་པ་དང་མི་ལྡན་པ་ཟང་ཟིང་མེད་པའི་ཚོར་བ། འདོད་ཡོན་ལྔ་ལ་སྲིད་པ་དང་མཚུངས་ལྡན་ཞེན་པ་རྟེན་པའི་ཚོར་བ། ཞེན་པ་མེད་པ་མངོན་འབྱུང་རྟེན་པའི་ཚོར་བ་སོགས་ཀྱི་རྣམ་གྲངས་ཡོད་དོ།

།འདུ་ཤེས་ནི་མཚན་མར་འཛིན་པ་སྟེ།

དེ་ལ་རྟེན་གྱི་སྒོ་ནས་དབྱེ་ན། མིག་གི་འདུས་ཏེ་རེག་པ་ལས་བྱུང་བའི་འདུ་ཤེས་སོགས་ཡིད་ཀྱི་བར་གྱི་དྲུག་གོ། །ཡང་དོན་ལ་མཚན་མར་འཛིན་པ་སྔོ་སེར་སོགས་སྣང་བ་འཛིན་པ། ཐ་སྙད་ལ་མཚན་མར་འཛིན་པ་སྐྱེས་པ་བུད་མེད་སོགས་སུ་རྟོག་པ་སྟེ། ནང་གི་དབྱེ་བ་ནི་ཤེས་བྱའི་གྲངས་སྙེད་དོ།

།ཡང་མཚན་མ་དང་བཅས་པའི་འདུ་ཤེས་ནི་ཐ་སྙད་ལ་མི་མཁས་པ་སྟེ་གཟུགས་མཐོང་ཡང་བརྡ་ལ་མ་བྱུང་བས་བརྡ་མི་ཤེས་པ་དང་། མཚན་མེད་ཀྱི་དབྱིངས་དང་། སྲིད་རྩེ་ལ་སྙོམས་པར་ཞུགས་པའི་འདུ་ཤེས་རྣམས་མ་གཏོགས་པ་དེ་ལས་གཞན་པའི་འདུ་ཤེས་ཐམས་ཅད་དོ།

མཚན་མ་མེད་པའི་འདུ་ཤེས་ནི་མ་གཏོགས་པ་དེ་དག་གོ།

།ཆུང་ངུའི་འདུ་ཤེས་ནི་གང་གིས་འདོད་ཁམས་ཤེས་པ།

[1,27] Moreover, there are various types such as physical sensations concurrent with the cognitions of the five sense doors; mental sensations concurrent with mental cognitions; turbulent sensations concurrent with physical craving; sensations free from turbulence which are not concurrent with craving; sensations that support clinging and are concurrent with craving for the five sense pleasures; and sensations that support deliverance and are free from clinging.

PERCEPTION

[1,28] Perceptions consist of the grasping of distinguishing features.

[1,29] In terms of support, they can be divided into six types: perceptions resulting from contact, the meeting of the eye and so forth, up until the mind.

Furthermore, there are the perceiving distinguishing features in regard to sense objects, such as perceiving an appearance as being blue, yellow and so forth; and perceiving distinguishing features in regard to names, such as perceiving man, woman and so forth as being such.

[1,30] There are as many subdivisions as there are knowable things. Moreover, perceptions can be divided into these six types:

1) Perceptions with characteristics are all the perceptions except for A) the perception of someone unskilled in conventional names, which means being unable, even when seeing a form, to name it because of not having learned its name; B) the perception of space without characteristics; and C) the perception of serenity at the summit of existence.

2) Perceptions without characteristics involve these [three] exceptions.

3) Lesser perceptions are perceptions that cause something to be perceived in the Desire Realms.

དེ་བཞིན་དུ་རྒྱ་ཆེན་པོའི་འདུ་ཤེས་ནི་གཟུགས་ཁམས་ཞེས་པ། ཚད་མེད་པའི་འདུ་ཤེས་ནི་ནམ་མཁའ་མཐའ་ཡས་དང་རྣམ་ཤེས་མཐའ་ཡས་ཞེས་པ། ཅི་ཡང་མེད་པའི་འདུ་ཤེས་ནི་ཅི་ཡང་མེད་པའི་སྐྱེ་མཆེད་ཞེས་པ་སྟེ་དྲུག་ཏུ་དབྱེ་བ་སོགས་སོ།

།འདུ་བྱེད་ཀྱི་ཕུང་པོ་ནི་མངོན་པར་འདུ་བྱེད་པའི་མཚན་ཉིད་ཅན། ཕུང་པོ་བཞི་ལས་གཞན་པའི་འདུས་བྱས་ཐམས་ཅད་ལ་བརྗོད་དེ།

དེ་ལ་སེམས་དང་མཚུངས་ལྡན་གྱི་འདུ་བྱེད་སེམས་བྱུང་རྣམས་དང་མཚུངས་ལྡན་མིན་པའི་འདུ་བྱེད་ཐོབ་པ་སོགས་ལྡན་མིན་འདུ་བྱེད་རྣམས་སོ།

།དེ་ཡང་སེམས་བྱུང་ལྔ་བཅུ་ང་གཅིག་ཡོད་ལ་ལྔ་བ་ལྔ་སོ་སོར་བསྡུ་ན་ང་ལྔར་འགྱུར་རོ།

།སེམས་བྱུང་ཀུན་འགྲོ་ལྔ་ནི། སེམས་པ་དང་ཚོར་བ་འདུ་ཤེས་ཡིད་ལ་བྱེད་པ་རེག་པ་ལྔ་ལས་ཚོར་འདུ་གཉིས་གོང་དུ་བཤད་ཟིན་ལ་དེ་དག་སེམས་བྱུང་ཡིན་ཀྱང་འདུ་བྱེད་ཀྱི་ཕུང་པོར་མི་བསྡུ་སྟེ་ལོགས་སུ་བཤད་པའི་ཕྱིར་རོ།

།སེམས་པ་ནི་སེམས་ཡུལ་ལ་གཡོ་ཞིང་འཇུག་པ་སྟེ། རྟེན་གྱི་སྒོ་ནས་མིག་གི་འདུས་ཏེ་སེམས་པ་སོགས་དྲུག་གོ།

།ཡིད་བྱེད་ནི་དམིགས་པ་ལ་སེམས་འཛིན་པ།

རེག་པ་ནི་གསུམ་འདུས་ནས་དབང་པོའི་འགྱུར་བ་ཡོངས་སུ་གཅོད་པ་ཚོར་བའི་རྟེན་བྱེད་པའོ།

4) Vast perceptions cause something to be perceived in the Form Realms.

5) Immeasurable perceptions cause [the spheres of] infinite space and of infinite consciousness to be perceived.

6) The perception of nothing whatsoever causes the sphere of nothing whatsoever to be perceived.

FORMATIONS

[1,31] The aggregate of formations is defined as the act of thoroughly creating. It is defined as all conditioned things other than the four aggregates [of form, sensation, perception and consciousness].

[1,32] This aggregate includes the formations concurrent with mind [a cognitive act] such as the [fifty-one] mental states, and the formations that are not concurrent with a cognitive act, the so-called nonconcurrent formations such as acquisition and so forth.

[1,33] There are fifty-one mental states, or fifty-five when the [five] views are counted individually:

[1,34] The five ever-present mental states are attraction, sensation, perception, attention, and contact. Among these, sensation and perception have been explained above. Although they are mental states, they are not included within the aggregate of formation because they have been taught separately.

[1,35] Attraction describes the process of mind [attention] moving towards and becoming involved with an object. In terms of support, there are six such as attraction upon the meeting of the eye [i.e. between object, sense faculty and consciousness], and so forth.

[1,36] Attention describes the process of the mind fixating upon the object concerned.

[1,37] Contact is the meeting together of the three [object, sense faculty and consciousness] and the cognition of the faculty's [particular] event. It supports sensation.

།འདི་ལྔ་སེམས་ཐམས་ཅད་ཀྱི་འཁོར་དུ་འབྱུང་བས་ཀུན་འགྲོ་ཞེས་བྱའོ།

།ཡུལ་ངེས་བྱེད་ལྔ་ནི། འདུན་པ་མོས་པ་དྲན་པ་ཏིང་འཛིན་ཤེས་རབ་བོ།

།དེ་ལ་འདུན་པ་ནི་འདོད་པའི་དངོས་པོ་ལ་དེ་དང་ལྡན་པར་བྱེད་པ་བརྩོན་འགྲུས་རྩོམ་པའི་རྟེན་བྱེད་པ། མོས་པ་ནི་ངེས་པའི་དངོས་པོ་ལ་དེ་བཞིན་དུ་འཛིན་པ་མི་འཕྲོག་པའི་བྱེད་ལས་ཅན་ནོ།

།དྲན་པ་ནི། འདྲིས་པའི་དོན་མི་བརྗེད་པ་མི་གཡེང་བའི་ལས་ཅན་ནོ།

།ཏིང་ངེ་འཛིན་ནི་བརྟག་པའི་དངོས་པོ་ལ་སེམས་རྩེ་གཅིག་པ་ཤེས་པའི་རྟེན་བྱེད་པའི་ལས་ཅན་ནོ།

།ཤེས་རབ་ནི་བརྟགས་པའི་ཆོས་རབ་ཏུ་རྣམ་པར་འབྱེད་པ་སྟེ་སོམ་ཉི་ཟློག་པའི་ལས་ཅན་ནོ།

།གོང་གི་བཅུ་པོ་འདི་ལ་སེམས་ཀྱི་ས་མང་པོ་བཅུ་ཞེས་བཤད་དོ།

།དགེ་བའི་སེམས་བྱུང་བཅུ་གཅིག་ལས།

དད་པ་ནི་ཡང་དག་པའི་གནས་ལ་དང་འདོད་ཡིད་ཆེས་པ་སྟེ་འདུན་པའི་རྟེན་བྱེད་པའོ།

།བག་ཡོད་པ་ནི་བླང་དོར་གྱི་གནས་ལ་གཟབ་པ་ལྷུར་ལེན་པ་སྲིད་ཞིའི་ལེགས་པ་སྒྲུབ་པའི་ལས་ཅན་ནོ། །ཤིན་ཏུ་སྦྱང་བ་ནི་ལུས་སེམས་དགེ་བ་ལ་བཀོལ་བཏུབ་པའི་ལས་སུ་རུང་བ་སྟེ་གནས་ངན་ལེན་འཇོམས་པའོ། །བཏང་སྙོམས་ནི་ཆགས་སྡང་གཏི་སྨུག་མེད་པར་སེམས་རྣལ་དུ་གནས་པ་སྟེ། ཉོན་མོངས་པའི་སྐབས་མི་འབྱེད་པའི་ལས་ཅན་ནོ།

།ངོ་ཚ་ཤེས་པ་ནི་བདག་གམ་ཆོས་རྒྱུ་མཚན་དུ་བྱས་ཏེ་ཁ་ན་མ་ཐོ་བ་ལ་འཛེམ་པ་ཉེས་སྤྱོད་སྡོམ་པའི་རྟེན་བྱེད་པའི་ལས་ཅན་ནོ།

[1,38] Since these five accompany all cognitive acts, they are called ever-present.

[1,39] The five object-determining [mental states] are intention, interest, recollection, concentration, and discrimination.

[1,40] Intention is to try to possess a desired object. It supports application of exertion.

[1,41] Interest means holding on to the certain form of a determined object. Its function is to not lose the object.

[1,42] Recollection means not forgetting a known object. Its function is to inhibit distraction.

[1,43] Concentration means to have one-pointed mind with regard to the examined object. Its function is to support [right] cognition.

[1,44] Discrimination means fully discerning the examined object. Its function is to cast away uncertainty.

[1,45] The above ten [mental states] are called the ten general mind bases.

[1,46] The eleven virtuous mental states:

[1,47] Faith is admiration of, longing towards, and trust in that which is true. It supports determination.

[1,48] Conscientiousness is the earnest application of care concerning what should be adopted and what should be abandoned. Its function is to accomplish the excellence of existence and quiescence [samsara and nirvana].

[1,49] Pliancy is the ability to apply body and mind to virtue. Its function is to overcome negative tendencies.

[1,50] Equanimity is the mind resting naturally, free from attachment, anger and delusion. Its function is to avoid giving occasion for the disturbing emotions [to occur in one's stream-of-being].

[1,51] Conscience means shunning misdeeds either because of oneself or the Dharma. Its function is to support one in refraining from negative actions.

།ཁྲེལ་ཡོད་པ་ནི་གཞན་ནམ་འཇིག་རྟེན་རྒྱུ་མཚན་དུ་བྱས་ཏེ་ཁ་ན་མ་ཐོ་བ་ལ་འཛེམ་པའི་ལས་ཅན་ནོ། །མ་ཆགས་པ་ནི་སྲིད་པ་དང་སྲིད་པའི་ཡོ་བྱད་ལ་མ་ཆགས་པ་སྟེ་ཉེས་སྤྱོད་ལ་མི་འཇུག་པར་བྱེད་པའོ།

།ཞེ་སྡང་མེད་པ་ནི་སེམས་ཅན་དང་སྡུག་བསྔལ་གྱི་ཆོས་ལ་ཀུན་ནས་མནར་སེམས་མེད་པ་སྟེ་ཉེས་སྤྱོད་ལ་མི་འཇུག་པར་བྱེད་པའོ།

།གཏི་མུག་མེད་པ་ནི་སོ་སོར་བརྟགས་པའི་བློ་ནས་དོན་ལ་མ་རྨོངས་པ་སྟེ་ཉེས་པ་ལ་མི་འཇུག་པར་བྱེད་པའོ། །རྣམ་པར་མི་འཚེ་བ་ནི་ཞེ་སྡང་མེད་པའི་ཆར་གཏོགས་པ་སྙིང་རྗེ་བའི་སེམས་ཏེ། གཞན་ལ་མཐོ་མི་བརྩམ་པའི་ལས་ཅན་ནོ།

།བརྩོན་འགྲུས་ནི་དགེ་བའི་གནས་ལ་སེམས་མངོན་པར་སྤྲོ་བས་འཇུག་པ་སྟེ། དགེ་བའི་ཕྱོགས་ཡོངས་སུ་སྒྲུབ་པར་བྱེད་པའོ།

མི་དགེ་བའི་སེམས་བྱུང་ལ་རྩ་བའི་ཉོན་མོངས་པ་དྲུག ཉེ་བའི་ཉོན་མོངས་པ་ཉི་ཤུ་ཡོད་པའི། དང་པོ་རྩ་ཉོན་དྲུག་གི་མ་རིག་པ་ནི་ལས་འབྲས་དང་བདེན་པ་དཀོན་མཆོག་རྣམས་ཀྱི་ཚུལ་མི་ཤེས་པ་སྟེ། ཀུན་ཉོན་རྣམས་འབྱུང་བར་བྱེད་པའོ།

།འདོད་ཆགས་ནི་ཁམས་གསུམ་པའི་ཟག་བཅས་ཀྱི་ཕུང་པོ་ལ་ཆགས་པ་སྟེ་སྲིད་པའི་སྡུག་བསྔལ་སྐྱེད་པར་བྱེད་པའོ། །འདི་ལ་འདོད་ཁམས་པའི་འདོད་ཆགས་ལ་འདོད་པའི་འདོད་ཆགས་དང་། ཁམས་གོང་མ་གཉིས་ཀྱི་འདོད་ཆགས་ལ་སྲིད་པའི་འདོད་ཆགས་ཞེས་གཉིས་སུ་ཡང་གསུངས་སོ། །ཁོང་ཁྲོ་བ་ནི་སེམས་ཅན་དང་སྡུག་བསྔལ་དང་སྡུག་བསྔལ་གྱི་གཞི་ལ་ཀུན་ནས་མནར་སེམས་པ་སྟེ། བདེ་བར་རེག་པ་ལ་མི་གནས་ཤིང་ཉེས་སྤྱོད་ཀྱི་རྟེན་བྱེད་པའོ།

[1,52] Shame has the function of causing one to shun misdeeds, either because of being reproached by other [noble] people or by the world.

[1,53] Non-attachment is the absence of desire towards [samsaric] existence or worldly things. It makes one not engage in negative actions.

[1,54] Non-aggression is the absence of a hostile attitude towards a sentient being or an object that causes pain. It makes one not become involved in negative actions.

[1,55] Non-delusion means being without delusion concerning what is true due to discrimination. It makes one not engage in evil deeds.

[1,56] Non-violence is a compassionate attitude belonging to non-aggression. Its function is to avoid causing harm to others

[1,57] Diligence is the attitude of gladly engaging in what is virtuous. It makes one fully accomplish what is virtuous.

[1,58] Within the non-virtuous mental states there are six root disturbing emotions and twenty subsidiary disturbing emotions.

[1,59] First, the six root disturbing emotions:

[1,60] Ignorance means not knowing the [law of] actions and their effects, the [four] truths, and the [virtues of the] Precious Ones. It causes all affliction to occur.

[1,61] Attachment is to be attached to the defiling aggregates of the three realms. It produces the pain of [samsaric] existence. It is taught that there are two [types of attachment]; the attachment of a person in the Desire Realms, called attachment of desire, and the attachment of the two Upper Realms, called attachment of existence.

[1,62] Anger is the hostile attitude towards a sentient being, a painful object, or pain [itself]. It makes one not abide in peace and creates the basis for negative action.

།ང་རྒྱལ་ནི་འཇིག་ལྟ་ལ་བརྟེན་ནས་སེམས་མཐོ་བའི་རྣམ་པར་ཁེངས་པ་སྟེ། གཞན་ལ་མ་གུས་པ་དང་སྡུག་བསྔལ་འབྱུང་བའི་རྟེན་བྱེད་པ་དེ་ལ་དབྱེ་ན་བདུན་ཡོད་དོ།

།ཐེ་ཚོམ་ནི་བདེན་པའི་དོན་ལ་ཡིད་གཉིས་ཟ་བ་སྟེ། དགེ་བའི་ཕྱོགས་ལ་མི་འཇུག་པའི་ལས་ཅན་ནོ། །ལྟ་བ་ཉོན་མོངས་ཅན་ཐམས་ཅད་ལྟ་བ་སྟེ། ལྟ་བ་ངན་པ་ཐམས་ཅད་ཀྱི་རྟེན་བྱེད་པའོ། དེ་ལྟར་རྩ་ཉོན་དྲུག་གོ།

།ལྟ་བ་དེ་ལ་དབྱེ་ན་ལྔ་སྟེ། འཇིག་ཚོགས་ལ་ལྟ་བ་ནི་ཉེ་བར་ལེན་པའི་ཕུང་པོ་ལྔ་ལ་བདག་དང་བདག་གི་བར་ལྟ་བ་སྟེ། ལྟ་བ་གཞན་གྱི་རྟེན་བྱེད་པའོ།

།མཐར་འཛིན་པའི་ལྟ་བ་ནི། བདག་གམ་ཕུང་པོ་ལྔ་ལ་རྟག་པ་དང་ཆད་པར་འཛིན་པ་སྟེ། དབུ་མའི་ལམ་གྱིས་ངེས་པར་འབྱུང་བ་ལ་བར་དུ་གཅོད་པའི་ལས་ཅན་ནོ།

།ལོག་པར་ལྟ་བ་ནི། ལས་རྒྱུ་འབྲས་སོགས་ཡོད་པའི་དོན་ལ་མེད་པར་ལྟ་བ་སྟེ། དགེ་རྩ་གཅོད་པར་བྱེད་པའི་ལས་ཅན་ནོ།

།ལྟ་བ་མཆོག་འཛིན་ནི་གོང་གི་ལྟ་བ་ངན་པ་གསུམ་དང་ལྟ་བའི་གནས་ཉེར་ལེན་གྱི་ཕུང་པོ་ལྔ་ལ་མཆོག་དང་དམ་པར་ལྟ་བ་སྟེ་ལྟ་ངན་ལ་མངོན་པར་ཞེན་པར་བྱེད་པའོ།

།ཚུལ་ཁྲིམས་དང་བརྟུལ་ཞུགས་མཆོག་འཛིན་ནི། འདག་གྲོལ་མ་ཡིན་པའི་ཚུལ་ཁྲིམས་དང་བརྟུལ་ཞུགས་དང་དེའི་གནས་ཕུང་ལྔ་ལ་འདག་གྲོལ་ངེས་འབྱིན་དུ་ལྟ་བ་སྟེ། ངལ་བ་འབྲས་བུ་མེད་པའི་ལས་ཅན་ནོ།

།མཆོག་འཛིན་གཉིས་པོ་འདིས་དངོས་པོའི་ཚུལ་ལ་ཕྱིན་ཅི་ལོག་ཏུ་ཞུགས་པའི་ལྟ་ངན་དང་། ཐར་པའི་ཐབས་མིན་པའི་ལམ་ངན་ལ་ཞེན་པ་ཀུན་ཀྱང་མཚོན་པར་བྱེད་དོ།

[1,63] Arrogance is the conceited attitude of superiority based on the belief in the [transitory] collection. It creates the basis for disrespecting others and for the occurrence of suffering. It can be divided into seven types.[9]

[1,64] Doubt means to be of two minds about the meaning of the [four] truths. Its function is to make one not engage in what is virtuous.

[1,65] Belief is the view of all kinds of disturbed discrimination. It forms the support for all unwholesome beliefs.

These were the six root disturbing emotions.

[1,66] When belief is subdivided, there are five types:

[1,67] The belief in the transitory collection is the belief in an "I" and a "my" within the five perpetuating aggregates. It forms the basis for the other [unwholesome] beliefs.

[1,68] The belief of holding extremes means regarding the self or the five aggregates to be permanent or discontinuous. Its function is to hinder emancipation by means of the Middle Path.

[1,69] Perverted belief means regarding an existing fact as being nonexistent: for instance, to disregard the cause and effect of actions. Its function is to cut the virtuous roots.

[1,70] Holding a belief to be paramount means regarding the above three unwholesome beliefs as well as the basis for these beliefs, the five perpetuating aggregates, as being paramount and sacred. It causes complete clinging to an unwholesome belief.

[1,71] Holding a discipline or ritual to be paramount is to believe that a non-purifying or non-liberating discipline or ritual as well as its basis, the five aggregates, is purifying, liberating or capable of causing emancipation. Its function is to cause pointless hardship.

[1,72] These two types of holding to be paramount illustrate all unwholesome beliefs of erroneously viewing the way things are, as

།ལྟ་བ་ལྔ་པོ་དེ་ཐམས་ཅད་ཤེས་རབ་ཉོན་མོངས་ཅན་ཡིན་ལ། ལྟ་བ་ལྔ་དང་ལྟ་མིན་ལྔ་སྟེ་རྩ་ཉོན་བཅུ་པོ་དེ་ལས། མཆོག་འཛིན་གཉིས་དང་ལོག་ལྟ་ཐེ་ཚོམ་བཞི་ཀུན་བཏགས་ཡིན་ཞིང་། ལྷག་མ་དྲུག་ལ་ཀུན་བཏགས་དང་ལྷན་སྐྱེས་གཉིས་ཡོད་དོ།

།ཉེ་ཉོན་ཉི་ཤུ་ལས། ཁྲོ་བ་ནི་ཁོང་ཁྲོ་འཕེལ་ཏེ་བརྡེག་པ་སོགས་གནོད་པ་དངོས་སུ་ཤོམ་པར་བྱེད་པའོ། །འཁོན་དུ་འཛིན་པ་ནི་ཁོང་ཁྲོ་བའི་ཆར་གཏོགས་པ་གནོད་པའི་བསམ་པ་རྒྱུན་མི་གཏོང་ཞིང་མི་བཟོད་པར་བྱེད་པའོ།

།འཚིག་པ་ནི་ཁྲོ་བ་དང་འཁོན་འཛིན་གྱི་རྒྱུ་ལས་མི་བཟོད་པར་ཚིག་རྩུབ་སྨྲ་བར་བྱེད་པའོ།

།རྣམ་པར་འཚེ་བ་ནི་ཁོང་ཁྲོའི་ཆར་གཏོགས་པ། སྙིང་བརྩེ་བ་མེད་པར་རྣམ་པར་མཐོ་བཙམ་པའི་ལས་ཅན་ནོ།

།ཕྲག་དོག་ནི་ཁོང་ཁྲོའི་ཆར་གཏོགས་པ། རང་རྙེད་བཀུར་སོགས་ལ་ཆགས་ནས་གཞན་གྱི་ཕུན་ཚོགས་ལ་མི་བཟོད་པར་སེམས་ཁོང་ནས་འཁྲུགས་པ། ཡིད་མི་བདེ་ཞིང་སེམས་རྣལ་དུ་མི་གནས་ལ་ཉེས་པའི་རྟེན་བྱེད་པའོ།

།གཡོ་ནི་རྙེད་བཀུར་སོགས་ལ་ཆགས་པས་རང་གི་ཉེས་པ་སྦས་ཏེ་ཉེས་རྒྱུན་སྐྱོང་བའི་སེམས་གྱུ་བ་ཆགས་སྡང་གཏི་མུག་གི་ཆར་གཏོགས་པ་སྐྱེ་ཡང་དག་པའི་གདམས་ངག་རྙེད་པའི་བར་དུ་གཅོད་པའོ།

།སྒྱུ་ནི་རྙེད་བཀུར་སོགས་ཀྱི་ཕྱིར་རང་ལ་མེད་པའི་ཡོན་ཏན་ཡོད་པར་འཆོས་ནས་བདེན་པ་མིན་པས་གཞན་སླུ་བྱེད་རྫོངས་ཆགས་ཀྱི་ཆར་གཏོགས་པ་ཉོན་མོངས་དང་ཉེ་ཉོན་གྱི་གྲོགས་བྱེད་ཅིང་ལོག་འཚོ་སྒྲུབ་པའི་རྟེན་བྱེད་པའོ།

well as all kinds of clinging to an unwholesome path which is not a means to emancipation.

These five beliefs are disturbed discrimination.

[1,73] Among these ten [root] disturbing emotions, the beliefs and the five non-beliefs, four are imputations: the two types of holding to be paramount, perverted belief, and doubt. The remaining six can be both innate and imputed.

[1,74] The twenty subsidiary disturbing emotions:

[1,75] Fury is the increase of anger. It causes one to prepare to harm others, such as by hitting them.

[1,76] Resentment belongs to the category of anger. It causes one to cling to an intention to cause harm, and to refrain from forgiving.

[1,77] Spite causes one to be unforgiving and utter harsh words out of fury or resentment.

[1,78] Hostility belongs to the category of anger. Its function is to be uncompassionate and cause harm.

[1,79] Envy belongs to the category of anger. It is a mental state that is deeply disturbed by the desire to obtain honor and gain for oneself, and by the inability to bear the excellence of others. It forms the support for unhappiness, for the mind's inability to rest in naturalness, and for negative actions.

[1,80] Hypocrisy is the deceitful attitude which perpetuates negativity, concealing one's own faults because of the desire for such things as honor and gain. It belongs to the categories of attachment, anger and delusion and obstructs obtaining true instructions.

[1,81] Pretense is to deceive others through what is untrue, pretending to possess virtuous qualities which one is not endowed with for the sake of such things as honor and gain. It belongs to the category of delusion and attachment, and forms the support for disturbing emotions and subsidiary disturbing emotions, as well as for leading a perverted life.

།ངོ་ཚ་མེད་པ་ནི་བདག་རྒྱུ་མཚན་དུ་བྱས་ཏེ་སྡིག་པ་ལ་མི་འཛེམ་པ་དུག་གསུམ་གྱི་ཆར་གཏོགས་པ་ཉོན་མོངས་དང་ཉེ་ཉོན་གྱི་གྲོགས་བྱེད་པའོ།

།ཁྲེལ་མེད་པ་ནི་གཞན་རྒྱུ་མཚན་དུ་བྱས་ཏེ་མི་དགེ་བའི་ཕྱོགས་ལ་འཛེམ་པ་མེད་པར་འཇུག་པ་དུག་གསུམ་གྱི་ཆར་གཏོགས་པ། ཉོན་མོངས་ཀུན་གྱི་གྲོགས་བྱེད་པའོ།

།འཆབ་པ་ནི་གཏི་མུག་དང་ཆགས་པའི་ཆར་གཏོགས་པ་ལེགས་པར་བསྐུལ་བ་ལ་མི་འཇུག་ཅིང་རང་གི་ཉེས་པ་སྦྲིབ་པར་འདོད་པ་སྟེ། འགྱོད་པ་དང་རེག་པར་མི་གནས་པའི་རྟེན་བྱེད་པའོ།

།སེར་སྣ་ནི་འདོད་ཆགས་ཀྱི་རྒྱུ་ལས་ཡོ་བྱད་སོགས་བདོག་པའི་དངོས་པོ་ལ་དམ་དུ་འཛིན་པ་སྟེ་ཡོ་བྱད་མི་བསྙུང་བར་བྱེད་པའོ།

།རྒྱགས་པ་ནི་ནད་མེད་པ་དང་ལང་ཚོ་སོགས་རང་རྒྱུད་ལ་ཡོད་པའི་ཟག་བཅས་ཀྱི་ཕུན་ཚོགས་གང་ཡང་རུང་བ་ལ་དགའ་ཞིང་ཆགས་པའི་སེམས་ཀྱིས་རང་མགུས་འཐེགས་པ་" སྦྲིང་བའི་དོན་ནོ "སྟེ། ཉོན་མོངས་དང་ཉེ་ཉོན་གྱི་རྟེན་བྱེད་པའོ།

།མ་དད་པ་ནི་གཏི་མུག་གི་ཆར་གཏོགས་པ་ཡང་དག་པའི་གནས་དང་དགེ་ཆོས་ལ་མི་མོས་པ་ལེ་ལོའི་རྟེན་བྱེད་པའོ།

།ལེ་ལོ་ནི་ཉལ་སྙེས་འཕྲུས་སོགས་ཀྱི་བདེ་བ་ལྟ་བུའི་བྱ་བ་ངན་པ་ལ་ཞེན་ནས་དགེ་བའི་ཕྱོགས་ལ་མི་སྤྲོ་ཞིང་འཇུག་པ་ལྷོད་པར་བྱེད་པ་བརྩོན་འགྲུས་ཀྱི་མི་མཐུན་ཕྱོགས་སོ།

།བག་མེད་པ་ནི་དུག་གསུམ་ལེ་ལོ་དང་བཅས་པའི་རྒྱུ་ལས་དགེ་སྡིག་བླང་དོར་ལ་གཟབ་པ་ལྷུར་མི་ལེན་པ་བག་ཡོད་པའི་མི་མཐུན་ཕྱོགས་ཏེ། མི་དགེ་འཕེལ་ཞིང་དགེ་བ་འགྲིབ་པའི་ལས་ཅན་ནོ།

[1,82] Lack of conscience means not shunning evil deeds on account of oneself. It belongs to the category of the three poisons and assists the disturbing emotions and subsidiary disturbing emotions.

[1,83] Shamelessness means to personally engage in what is unvirtuous without inhibition on account of others. It belongs to the categories of the three poisons and helps all the disturbing emotions.

[1,84] Concealment belongs to the categories of delusion and attachment. It means not to engage in what has been fully warned about and to desire to cover up for one's faults. It forms the support for not feeling regret.

[1,85] Stinginess is to hold tightly onto possessed objects such as utensils and so forth because of attachment. It causes the inability to part with one's possessions.

[1,86] Self-infatuation is to have excessive pride and vanity due to fascination with or attachment towards any kind of conditioned prosperity possessed by oneself, such as good health or youthfulness. It forms the support for the disturbing emotions and subsidiary disturbing emotions.

[1,87] Lack of faith belongs in the category of delusion. It is to not be interested in what is true and virtuous. It forms the support for laziness.

[1,88] Laziness is to cling to unwholesome activities such as lying down, resting, or stretching out, and to procrastinate, without taking delight in and engaging in what is virtuous. It is the opponent of diligence.

[1,89] Heedlessness is not to apply oneself earnestly and carefully to adopting virtue and abandoning evil deeds, and is due to the three poisons along with laziness. It is the opponent of conscientiousness, and its function is to increase nonvirtue and to diminish virtue.

།བརྗེད་ངས་ནི་དགེ་བའི་དམིགས་པ་མི་གསལ་བར་བརྗེད་པ། དྲན་པའི་མི་མཐུན་ཕྱོགས་སུ་གྱུར་པའི་ཉོན་མོངས་དང་མཚུངས་ལྡན་གྱི་དྲན་པ་འཆལ་པ་སེམས་གཡེང་བའི་རྟེན་བྱེད་པའོ།

།ཤེས་བཞིན་མིན་པ་ནི་ཉོན་མོངས་དང་མཚུངས་པར་ལྡན་པ་གཡེང་བའི་ཤེས་རབ་སྟེ། སྒོ་གསུམ་གྱི་སྤྱོད་པ་ལ་ཤེས་བཞིན་དུ་མི་འཇུག་པར་བབ་བབ་དུ་འཇུག་པ་སྟེ་ལྟུང་བ་འབྱུང་བའི་རྟེན་བྱེད་པའོ།

།རྒྱགས་པ་ནི་གཏི་མུག་གི་ཆར་གཏོགས་པ་ལུས་སེམས་ལྕི་བའི་རྣམ་པས་དམིགས་པ་ལ་འཇུག་མི་ནུས་པར་ནང་དུ་སྡུད་ཅིང་སེམས་ལས་སུ་མི་རུང་བ་ཉོན་མོངས་པའི་རྟེན་བྱེད་པའོ།

།རྒོད་པ་ནི་སྡུག་པའི་མཚན་མའི་རྗེས་སུ་ཞུགས་པའི་འདོད་ཆགས་ཀྱི་ཆར་གཏོགས་པ་སེམས་ཡུལ་ལ་འཕྲོ་བས་ལས་སུ་མི་རུང་ཞིང་མ་ཞི་བར་བྱེད་པ་ཞི་གནས་ཀྱི་བར་དུ་གཅོད་པའོ།

།རྣམ་པར་གཡེང་བ་ནི་དུག་གསུམ་གྱི་ཆར་གཏོགས་པ་སེམས་ཡུལ་ལ་གཡོ་ཞིང་འཕྲུན་ཏེ་དགེ་བའི་དམིགས་པ་ལ་རྩེ་གཅིག་ཏུ་མི་གནས་པར་བྱེད་པ་སྟེ། འདི་ལ་ཕྱི་ནང་དང་མཚན་མའི་གཡེང་བ་སོགས་ཀྱི་དབྱེ་བ་ཡོད་དོ།

དེ་ལྟར་ཉི་ཤུ་ནི་རྩ་ཉོན་གྱི་ཆར་གཏོགས་ཤིང་དེ་དང་ཉེ་བས་ཉེ་ཉོན་ཞེས་བྱའོ།

།གཞན་འགྱུར་བཞི་ལས་གཉིད་ནི་གཉིད་ཀྱི་རྒྱུ་ལ་བརྟེན་ནས་དགེ་མི་དགེ་རིགས་མི་རིགས་དུས་དུས་མིན་སོགས་ཀྱི་རྣམ་འབྱེད་མེད་པར་སྒོ་ལྔའི་ཤེས་པ་ནང་དུ་སྡུད་པར་བྱེད་པ་གཏི་མུག་གི་ཆར་གཏོགས་པ་བྱ་བ་ཞོར་བའི་རྟེན་བྱེད་པའོ།

།འགྱོད་པ་ནི་སྔར་བྱས་པ་ལ་ཡིད་མི་དགའ་བའི་རྣམ་པས་ཡིད་ལ་བཅག་པ་སེམས་གནས་པའི་བར་དུ་གཅོད་པར་བྱེད་པའོ།

[1,90] Forgetfulness is to be unclear and forget a virtuous objective. It is the erroneous mindfulness which accompanies a disturbing emotion, and is the opponent of being mindful. It forms the support for distraction of mind.

[1,91] Non-alertness [inattention] is the distracted discrimination accompanying a disturbing emotion. It results in hasty and mindless engagement in the actions of the three doors without alertness, and so forms the support for downfalls to occur.

[1,92] Lethargy belongs to the category of delusion. It means to be withdrawn, mentally incapable, and unable to focus on an object because of heaviness of body and mind. It forms the support for the disturbing emotions.

[1,93] Excitement is the fascination with an attractive object and belongs to the category of desire. It is a mental incapacity due to the mind moving towards an object, and it causes restlessness. It is a hindrance to calm abiding.

[1,94] Distraction belongs to the categories of the three poisons. It is the mental motion or wandering towards an object which causes the inability to remain one-pointedly on a virtuous objective. It can be defined as distraction towards the outer, the inner, and towards status.

[1,95] These twenty belong to the categories of the root disturbing emotions; because of being associated with them, they are called subsidiary disturbing emotions.

[1,96] The four variables:

[1,97] Sleep causes the consciousnesses of the five sense doors to be withdrawn inwardly without any discrimination as to what is virtuous or unvirtuous, appropriate or inappropriate, or timely or untimely. It belongs to the category of delusion and forms the support for losing activities.

[1,98] Regret involves sadness because of mental displeasure with a former action. It obstructs resting the mind.

།རྟོག་པ་ནི་སེམས་པ་དང་ཤེས་རབ་ལ་བརྟེན་ནས་དམིགས་པའི་དངོས་པོ་ཀུན་ཏུ་ཚོལ་བའི་ཡིད་ཀྱིས་བརྗོད་པ་སྟེ། ངོ་བོ་ལ་སྤྱི་ཙམ་འཛིན་པ་རྩིང་བའི་རྣམ་པ་ཅན། རྒྱུད་རིང་པོའི་གཟུགས་ལ་ཁམ་ཕོར་དང་བུམ་པའི་ཁྱད་མ་ཕྱེ་བར་དེ་ཙམ་འཛིན་པ་ལྟ་བུའོ། །དཔྱོད་པ་ནི་སེམས་པ་དང་ཤེས་རབ་ལ་བརྟེན་ནས་དོན་དེའི་ཁྱད་པར་སོ་སོར་རྟོག་པའི་ཡིད་ཀྱིས་གཞིག་ནས་བརྟུང་བ་ཞིབ་པའི་རྣམ་པ་ཅན་དེ་བུམ་པ་གསར་པ་མ་གས་པར་འཛིན་པ་ལྟ་བུའོ། །དེ་རྣམས་ཀུན་སློང་དང་བསམ་པའི་ཁྱད་པར་གྱིས་དགེ་སྡིག་ལུང་མ་བསྟན་ཅི་རིགས་པར་འགྱུར་བས་གཞན་འགྱུར་བཞི་ཞེས་བྱའོ། །སེམས་བྱུང་འདི་དག་གིས་སྤྱིར་སེམས་ཀྱི་ས་མང་དང་། དགེ་སྡིག་གི་སེམས་བྱུང་རྣམས་ཀྱི་ཁྱད་པར་འབྱེད་པའི་གཙོ་བོར་འདི་ཙམ་གསུངས་ཞིང་། གཞན་ཡང་སེམས་པ་དང་འདུ་ཤེས་སོགས་ཀྱི་འཛིན་སྟངས་ཀྱི་ཁྱད་པར་ལས། སྐྱོ་བ་དང་མི་སྐྱོ་བ། དགའ་བ་དང་མི་དགའ་བ། བཟོད་པ་དང་མི་བཟོད་པ་སོགས་རྣམ་གྲངས་ཤིན་ཏུ་མང་པོར་འགྱུར་བ་ཤེས་པར་བྱའོ། དེ་རྣམས་ནི་སེམས་དང་མཚུངས་ལྡན་གྱི་འདུ་བྱེད་དོ།

།སེམས་བྱུང་ལྟ་བུའི་འདུ་བྱེད་མིན་ཡང་འདུས་བྱས་སུ་ནི་གཏོགས་དགོས་ཤིང་བེམ་ཤེས་གང་རུང་དུ་བསྡུ་བར་མི་འོས་པའི་ཆོས་ལ་སེམས་དང་མཚུངས་པར་ལྡན་པ་མིན་པའི་འདུ་བྱེད་ཀྱི་ཆོས་ཡིན་པ་ཞེས་བྱའོ། དེ་ལྟར་བེམ་ཤེས་ལྡན་མིན་གསུམ་གྱིས་འདུས་བྱས་ཐམས་ཅད་བསྡུས་པར་རིག་པར་བྱ་སྟེ། རྟུལ་དུ་གྲུབ་པ་བེམ་པོའོ། །གསལ་ཞིང་རིག་པ་ཤེས་པའོ། །དེ་གཉིས་མ་ཡིན་པའི་འདུས་བྱས་ཐམས་ཅད་ལྡན་མིན་འདུ་བྱེད་དོ།

།ལྡན་མིན་འདུ་བྱེད་དེ་གང་ཞེ་ན། རང་གི་རྒྱུད་ལ་དགེ་མི་དགེ་ལུང་མ་བསྟན་གྱི་ཆོས་གང་ཞིག་སྔར་མེད་གསར་དུ་ཐོབ་པ་དང་ཐོབ་པ་དེའི་རྒྱུན་ལྡན་པ་ལ་ཐོབ་པ་ཞེས་པ་སྟེ། རྒྱུད་དུ་གཏོགས་པའི་ཆོས་ཡིན་ལ་འདུས་བྱས་ཀྱང་ཡིན་པས་ལྡན་མིན་འདུ་བྱེད་ཅེས་བྱའོ།

[1,99] Conception is a mental expression created by the mind's investigation of an observed object by means of apprehension and discrimination. It is merely grasping a rough meaning and it has a coarse form, just like perceiving a distant form without distinguishing whether it is a clay bowl or a vase.

[1,100] Discernment is the action of the mind examining and taking hold of an object, and is capable of distinguishing the attributes of an object by means of apprehension and discrimination. It has a fine form, like distinguishing whether the vase is new or not.

[1,101] Since these can be changed into any kind of virtuous, negative or neutral form by the different attitudes or intents, they are called the four variables.

[1,102] With these mental states are mainly stated the distinctions of the general mind bases and the virtuous and negative mental states. It should be understood, however, that there are a tremendous number of different kinds, such as sadness and elation, difficulty and ease, patience and impatience, and so forth, which result from the different kinds of grasping patterns of apprehension, perception and so on.

All of these are formations concurrent with mind.

[1,103] Although it is not a formation like a mental state, a dharma which must belong to the category of formation and is not suitable for inclusion within either matter or mind is called a formation not concurrent with mind.

[1,104] It should thus be understood that all conditioned things are included within matter, mind and the nonconcurrent [formations]. Matter is what is made of particles. Mind is what is conscious and cognizant. Nonconcurrent formations are all the conditioned things which are neither of these.

[1,105] What is a nonconcurrent formation? [For example,] if a quality or attribute in one's being, whether virtuous, unvirtuous or neutral, is obtained anew without being there formerly, this

།དེ་བཞིན་དུ་དགེ་སོགས་རང་རྒྱུད་ལ་ཐོབ་པ་ལས་ཉམས་ཏེ་འགྲིབ་པར་གྱུར་བ་ལ་མ་ཐོབ་པ་ཞེས་བྱའོ།

།སེམས་ཅན་སོ་སོའི་རིས་སུ་སྐྱེས་ཏེ་སྐལ་པ་མཉམ་པའི་ཆོས་དེ་ལ་སྐལ་མཉམ་མམ་རིས་མཐུན་པ་ཞེས་བྱའོ།

།འདུ་ཤེས་མེད་པའི་སྙོམས་འཇུག་ནི་དགེ་རྒྱས་ཀྱི་འདོད་ཆགས་དང་བྲལ་ལ་ཁམས་གོང་མའི་འདོད་ཆགས་དང་མ་བྲལ་བ་ཞིག་གིས་ཡིད་ལ་བྱེད་པའི་སྒོ་ནས་སེམས་སེམས་བྱུང་རྒྱུན་བརྟན་པ་མ་ཡིན་པ་འཇུག་ཤེས་དྲུག་པོ་རྣམས་གནས་སྐབས་སུ་འགོག་པར་བྱེད་པ་སྟེ། སེམས་སེམས་བྱུང་ཁེགས་པའི་གནས་སྐབས་དེ་ལྟ་བུ་སྙོམས་འཇོག་གི་ནུས་པས་སྔོན་མེད་གསར་དུ་ཐོབ་ཅིང་། ཡང་དེ་ལས་ལྡང་ཏེ་འགག་པའི་ཕྱིར་སྐྱེ་འགག་ཡོད་ཀྱང་དེ་བེམ་ཤེས་གང་ཡང་མིན་པའི་ཆོས་ཡིན་པས་ལྡན་མིན་འདུ་བྱེད་དུ་བཞག་གོ།

།དེ་བཞིན་དུ་སྙོམས་འཇུག་དེས་འཕངས་ནས་འདུ་ཤེས་མེད་པའི་ལྷ་རྣམས་ཀྱི་ནང་དུ་སྐྱེས་པ་འདུ་ཤེས་མེད་པ་པ་དང་།

འགོག་པའི་སྙོམས་འཇུག་ནི་སྲིད་རྩེའི་སེམས་ལས་གྱེན་དུ་བསྐྱོད་དེ་བདག་མེད་པ་དང་ཞི་གནས་ཀྱི་འདུ་ཤེས་སྔོན་དུ་བཏང་བས་སེམས་བྱུང་བརྟན་པ་མིན་པ་རྣམས་དང་བརྟན་པ་ལས་ཁ་ཅིག་སྟེ། ཉོན་ཡིད་ཀྱིས་བསྡུས་པ་རྣམས་ཁེགས་པའོ།

།འདི་གསུམ་ལྡན་མིན་འདུ་བྱེད་དུ་འཇོག་པའི་སྐབས་ན་ཇི་སྲིད་སེམས་སེམས་བྱུང་འགོག་པའི་ནུས་པ་དེ་ལ་གོ་དགོས་སོ།

possession being [now] continuously present is called acquisition. So, that which is an attribute belonging to one's being and which also is a conditioned thing is called a nonconcurrent formation.

[1,106] In the same way, something such as a virtue which is diminished or degenerated from being an acquisition in one's being is called a dispossession.

[1,107] For those born in one of the different classes of sentient beings, the quality of belonging to the same kind of species is called same status or similar class.

[1,108] Perceptionless serenity is that which, being free from attachment to the abode of Full Beauty but not free from the attachment of the realms above, is not a steady continuance of mind and mental states. It is the temporary bringing to cessation of all the six kinds of engaged cognitions. Such a period where mind and mental states are blocked is a new acquisition through the power of serenity which was not formerly present. Since it will again cease when emerging from that serenity, it has an arising and a ceasing, yet it is a quality which is neither mind nor matter and is therefore defined as a nonconcurrent formation.

[1,109] In this way, having been impelled by this serenity, one is born among the perceptionless gods. That is called [a state of] non-perception.

[1,110] The serenity of cessation is, preceded by the perception of non-self and calm abiding, to move upward from the state of mind of the summit of existence. Therefore it involves the blocking of all inconstant mental states and, among the constant ones, all that consists of disturbed mental cognition.

[1,111] When defining these three as being nonconcurrent formations it should be understood that they have the power to endure as long as mind and mental states have cessed.

།བརྟན་པ་ཀུན་གཞི་ནི་འདུ་ཤེས་མེད་པ་པ་དང་སྙོམས་འཇུག་གཉིས་ཀྱིས་མི་ཁེགས་ཏེ་དེའི་དབང་གིས་སེམས་སླར་ཡང་སྐྱེས་བར་རུང་ངོ་།

།སྲོག་གི་དབང་པོ་ནི་སེམས་ཅན་རིས་མཐུན་པར་སྔོན་ལས་ཀྱི་དབང་གིས་ཅི་ཙམ་གནས་པའི་དུས་ངེས་པ་ཚེ་ཞེས་བརྗོད་པ་གང་ཡིན་པའོ།

།སྐྱེ་བ་ནི་འདུ་བྱེད་རྣམས་སྔར་མ་བྱུང་བ་ལས་ད་ལྟར་བྱུང་བའོ།

།གནས་པ་ནི་དེའི་རྒྱུན་གནས་པའོ།

།རྒ་བ་ནི་རྒྱུན་གཞན་དུ་འགྱུར་བའོ།

།མི་རྟག་པ་ནི་རྒྱུན་འཇིག་པ་སྟེ་འདི་བཞི་ལ་འདུས་བྱས་སུ་མཚོན་པའི་མཚན་ཉིད་བཞི་ཞེས་བྱའོ།

།མིང་གི་ཚོགས་ནི་ཀ་བུམ་སོགས་དོན་གྱི་ངོ་བོ་ཙམ་བརྗོད་པའི་བརྡའོ།

།ཚིག་གི་ཚོགས་ནི་དོན་གྱི་ངོ་བོ་དང་ཁྱད་པར་སྦྱར་ཏེ་སྟོན་པར་བྱེད་པའི་བླ་དྭགས་སོ།

།ཡི་གེའི་ཚོགས་ནི་མིང་ཚིག་གཉིས་ཀྱི་རྩོམ་གཞིར་གྱུར་པའི་ཡིག་འབྲུ་ཨ་ལ་སོགས་པའོ།

།འདི་གསུམ་སྐད་གདངས་ཀྱིས་བསྡུས་ན་ཡང་སྒྲ་ཙམ་དང་མི་འདྲ་བའི་ཁྱད་པར་སེམས་ཀྱི་བརྟར་བཏགས་ནས་བརྗོད་བྱ་ལུང་སྟོན་པ་སོགས་ཀྱི་ནུས་པ་ཅན་འདུ་བྱེད་ཀྱི་ཆོས་སུ་གཏོགས་པའོ། །མངོན་པ་མཛོད་ལས་བཅུ་བཞི་པོ་འདི་ཙམ་གསུངས་སོ།

།མངོན་པ་ཀུན་བཏུས་ལས་སྔ་མ་བཅུ་བཞིའི་སྟེང་དུ།

སོ་སོའི་སྐྱེ་བོ་ནི་འཕགས་པའི་ཆོས་མ་ཐོབ་པའོ། འདི་ནི་ཐེམ་ཤེས་ལྡན་པ་ལ་བཏགས་པའི་གང་ཟག་གི་བྱེ་བྲག་གོ།

[1,112] The ongoing all-ground is not blocked by the [state of] non-perception and the two types of serenity, and because of this, a cognitive act is again liable to occur.

[1,113] The life faculty is what is called life span for a similar class of sentient beings: the particular length of time they can remain through the power of former karma.

[1,114] Birth is the present occurrence of all formations which did not occur previously.

[1,115] Subsistence is the remaining of that continuity.

[1,116] Aging is the change of that continuity into something else.

[1,117] Impermanence is the destruction of that continuity.

[1,118] These four are called the four characteristics that indicate a conditioned thing.

[1,119] The category of names consists of the indications that simply express the identity of an object such as 'pillar' or 'vase'.

[1,120] The category of words are the names that show the identity of an object joined with its particularities.

[1,121] The category of letters are the syllables such as 'A' which are the basis for composing both names and words.

[1,122] When these three are combined by a voice, mere sounds and their particularities can be mentally labeled and thus have the capacity to state or express things. They belong to the dharmas of formations.

This number [of fourteen nonconcurrent formations] is what is mentioned in the *Abhidharma Kosha*.

[1,123] According to the *Abhidharma Samucchaya*, there are in addition to the above fourteen [nonconcurrent formations] also:

[1,124] Ordinary person is the [state of] not having acquired the qualities of a noble being. It is a particular type of person, a labeling on the possession of mind and matter.

།འཇུག་པ་ནི་རྒྱུ་དང་འབྲས་བུ་རྒྱུན་མི་འཆད་པར་འཇུག་པའོ།

།སོ་སོར་ངེས་པ་ནི་རྒྱུ་དང་འབྲས་བུ་ཐ་དད་པའོ།

།འབྱོར་འབྲེལ་བ་ནི་རྒྱུ་དང་འབྲས་བུ་རྗེས་སུ་མཐུན་པའོ།

།མགྱོགས་པ་ནི་རྒྱུ་དང་འབྲས་བུ་མྱུར་བར་འབྱུང་བའོ།

།གོ་རིམ་ནི་རྒྱུ་དང་འབྲས་བུ་རེ་རེ་ནས་རིམ་བཞིན་འབྱུང་བའོ།

།དུས་ནི་རྒྱུ་དང་འབྲས་བུ་རྒྱུན་དུ་འབྱུང་བའི་ཡུན་གྱི་གནས་སྐབས་སོ།

།ཡུལ་ནི་ཕྱོགས་བཅུ་པོ་ཐམས་ཅད་ན་རྒྱུ་དང་འབྲས་བུ་ཡོད་པ་ལས་བཏགས་པའོ།

།གྲངས་ནི་འདུ་བྱེད་རྣམས་སོ་སོ་ཐ་དད་པ་ལ་བགྲངས་ཏེ་བཞག་པའོ།

།ཚོགས་པ་ནི་རྒྱུ་དང་འབྲས་བུའི་རྐྱེན་འདུས་པའི་གནས་སྐབས་ལས་སོ།

།ཅིར་བཞི་པོ་འདི་དག་གིས་མཚོན་ནས་ཐེམ་ཤེས་ཀྱི་གནས་སྐབས་ལ་བཏགས་པའི་ཆོས་འདུས་ཁྱུས་སུ་བསྡུ་དགོས་ལ་ཐེམ་ཤེས་གང་དུ་བསྡུར་མི་འོངས་པ་དུ་མ་ཡོད་པ་ཤེས་པར་བྱའོ།

།རྣམ་པར་ཤེས་པའི་ཕུང་པོ་ནི། ཆོས་རྣམས་ཀྱི་དོན་གྱི་ངོ་བོ་སོ་སོར་རིག་པར་བྱེད་པ་སྟེ་དེ་ལ་དབྱེ་ན།

མིག་གི་རྣམ་པར་ཤེས་པ་ནས། ཡིད་ཀྱི་རྣམ་པར་ཤེས་པའི་བར་གྱི་ཚོགས་དྲུག་ནི། བདག་རྐྱེན་མིག་གི་དབང་པོ་ལ་བརྟེན་ནས་སྐྱེས་པའི་བློ་གང་གིས་གཟུགས་ཤེས་པ་ནས། བདག་རྐྱེན་ཡིད་དབང་ལ་བརྟེན་ནས་སྐྱེས་པའི་བློ་གང་གིས་རང་ཡུལ་ཐུན་མིན་ཆོས་ཁམས་དང་དེ་ལས་གཞན་པ་རྣམས་ཀྱང་ཤེས་པའི་བར་དུའོ།

[1,125] Regular sequence is the uninterrupted continuance of cause and effect.

[1,126] Definitive distinctiveness is the difference between causes and effects.

[1,127] Connected link is the relatedness between cause and effects.

[1,128] Speed is the rapid occurrence of cause and effect.

[1,129] Sequence is the gradual occurrence of individual causes and effects.

[1,130] Time is the duration of occurrence of a continuity of a cause and effect.

[1,131] Location is the name of the ten directions from the existence of cause and effect in any of them.

[1,132] Number is the system of enumerating all the individual and different formations.

[1,133] Gathering is the time when the conditions for cause and effect have come together.

[1,134] As shown by these twenty-four [nonconcurrent formations], dharmas labeled at the occasion of mind and matter should be grouped under conditioned things, and it should be understood that there are many that belong to neither mind nor matter.

THE AGGREGATE OF CONSCIOUSNESS

[1,135] The aggregate of consciousness is that which individually cognizes the object-identity of all phenomena.

[1,136] This aggregate can be divided into the six collections from visual cognition to mental cognition. They are [the six] from the cognition of form by a cognitive act that has occurred by means of the ruling condition of the eye faculty up until the cognition of its own special object, the element of mental objects as well as the other objects, by a cognitive act that has occurred by means of the ruling condition of the mind faculty.

།སེམས་ཙམ་གྱི་མདོ་དང་བསྟན་བཅོས་ལས་ཚོགས་བརྒྱད་དུ་བཞེད་དེ།

ཡིད་ཤེས་ཀྱི་བྱེ་བྲག་རྟག་ཏུ་རློམ་སེམས་པ་གང་ཞིག ནང་དུ་ཀུན་གཞིའི་རྣམ་ཤེས་ལ་དམིགས་ནས། བདག་ཏུ་ལྟ་བ་དང་། ངའོ་སྙམ་པའི་ང་རྒྱལ་དང་། བདག་ཏུ་ཆགས་པ་དང་། མ་རིག་པ་སྟེ་ཉོན་མོངས་བཞི་པོ་དང་མཚུངས་པར་ལྡན་པའི་སེམས་དེ་ནི། འཕགས་ལམ་མངོན་གྱུར་དང་། འགོག་པའི་སྙོམས་འཇུག་དང་། མི་སློབ་པའི་ས་མ་གཏོགས་པར་དགེ་མི་དགེ་ལུང་མ་བསྟན་གྱི་སེམས་ཐམས་ཅད་དུ་འགྲོ་བ་ལ་ཉོན་མོངས་པའི་ཡིད་ཅེས་བྱའོ།

།ཀུན་གཞིའི་རྣམ་ཤེས་ནི་ཕུང་ཁམས་སྐྱེ་མཆེད་ཀྱིས་ཡོངས་སུ་བསྡོམས་པའི་ས་བོན་ཐམས་ཅད་པ་འཛིན་པ་སེམས་ཀྱི་གཞི་གསལ་རིག་ཙམ་རིས་སུ་མ་ཆད་པ་སྟེ། འདི་ལ་གནས་དོན་ལུས་སུ་སྣང་བ་འབྱུང་རུང་གི་ས་བོན་ཙམ་དུ་གནས་པའི་ཆ་ནས་ཀུན་གཞི་དང་ལེན་པའི་རྣམ་པར་ཤེས་པ་ཞེས་ཀྱང་བྱ། གནས་དོན་ལུས་སུ་སྣང་ཡང་རྨི་ལམ་གྱི་སྣང་བ་ལྟར་ཀུན་གཞིའི་རྣམ་ཤེས་ཉིད་དེར་སྣང་བ་ཙམ་དུ་ཟད་པའི་ཆ་ནས་རྣམ་པར་སྨིན་པའི་ཀུན་གཞི་འམ་དེའི་རྣམ་ཤེས་ཞེས་ཀྱང་བྱའོ།

།སེམས་དང་ཡིད་དང་རྣམ་ཤེས་ནི་དོན་གཅིག་མིང་གི་རྣམ་གྲངས་ཙམ་དུ་བཞེད་པ་ཡོད་ལ། ཡང་སེམས་ཀུན་གཞིའི་རྣམ་ཤེས། ཡིད་ཉོན་མོངས་པའི་ཡིད། རྣམ་པར་ཤེས་པ་ཚོགས་དྲུག་གི་མིང་དུ་བཞེད་དོ།

།དེ་ལྟར་ཕུང་པོ་ལྔ་པོ་དེས་འདུས་བྱས་ཀྱི་ཆོས་ཐམས་ཅད་བསྡུས་པའི་ཕྱིར་ན། དེ་ལས་བརྩམས་ཏེ་དུས་ལ་སོགས་པ་རྣམ་གྲངས་དང་རྣམ་བཞག་མང་པོ་འབྱུང་བའི་གཞི་ཡིན་པས། ཕུང་པོ་ལྔ་པོ་དེ་ལ་དུས་དང་གཏམ་གྱི་གཞི་དང་། ངེས་པར་འབྱུང་བ་དང་བཅས་པ། རྒྱུ་དང་བཅས་པ་ཞེས་ཟེར་ཞིང་། འཇིག་རྟེན་དང་ལྟ་བའི་གནས་དང་སྲིད་པ་ཞེས་ཀྱང་བྱའོ།

[1,137] In the sutras and treatises of Mind Only it is held that there are eight collections [of cognitions]:

[1,138] The disturbed mental cognition is the aspect of the mind consciousness which is constantly conceited [with the idea "I am"] and which inwardly uses as reference the all-ground consciousness. It is the [aspect of] mind concurrent with the four disturbing emotions of belief in a self, the arrogance of thinking "I am," attachment to a self, and ignorance. Apart from the actualization of the path of noble beings, the serenity of cessation, and the state of no-learning, it accompanies all cognitive acts whether they be virtuous, unvirtuous or neutral.

[1,139] The all-ground consciousness is the holder of all the seeds implanted by the aggregates, elements, and sources. It is the basis for cognitive acts and, without bias, it is merely cognizant and conscious.

Due to the fact of being merely the seed for environment, sense objects, and a body to appear, it is also called all-ground and perpetuating consciousness. Since whatever is experienced as environment, sense objects and a body is merely the all-ground consciousness appearing as that, just like a dream experience, it is also called all-ground of maturation or the all-ground consciousness of maturation.

[1,140] One viewpoint maintains that cognitive act, mental faculty [mind] and consciousness are merely synonyms for the same meaning. Yet, it is held that cognitive act is the term for the all-ground consciousness, mental faculty for the disturbed mental cognition, and consciousness for the six collections.

[1,141] In this way, all phenomena which are conditioned things are included within these five aggregates. They are the basis from which many systems come about, such as time and so forth. The five aggregates are therefore called the basis for discourse and

།འདུན་པ་དང་འདོད་ཆགས་ཀྱི་སྒོ་ནས་ཉེ་བར་ལེན་པས་ཟག་བཅས་ཉེར་ལེན་གྱི་ཕུང་པོ་ལ་ནི་འཐབ་པ་དང་བཅས་པ་དང་སྡུག་བསྔལ་དང་ཀུན་འབྱུང་ཞེས་ཀྱང་བྱའོ།

།ཕུང་པོའི་རབ་ཏུ་དབྱེ་བའི་སྐབས་སོ།

time, the basis for renunciation and the basis for the causes. They are also called the world, the ground of beliefs, and existence.

[1,142] By means of intention and desire the [five aggregates] are perpetuating causes. So, these aggregates that perpetuate defilements are also named basis for strife, suffering, and origin [of suffering].

[1,143] This was the chapter on the presentation of the aggregates.

ཁམས་བཅོ་བརྒྱད་ནི། གཟུགས་ཀྱི་ཕུང་པོ་ལས་ཁམས་བཅུ་བཞག་སྟེ། གང་ཞེ་ན་མིག་གི་ཁམས་ནས་ལུས་ཁམས་ཀྱི་བར་ལྔ་དང་། གཟུགས་ནས་རེག་བྱའི་བར་གྱི་ཁམས་ལྔ་སྟེ་བཅུ་འོ།

།རྣམ་པར་ཤེས་པའི་ཁམས་བདུན་ཏེ་མིག་གི་རྣམ་ཤེས་ཀྱི་ཁམས་ནས་ཡིད་ཀྱི་རྣམ་ཤེས་ཀྱི་ཁམས་ཀྱི་བར་དྲུག་དང་། ཡིད་ཀྱི་ཁམས་དང་བདུན་ནོ།

།ཡིད་ཀྱི་ཁམས་ཞེས་པ་ཡིད་ཀྱི་དབང་པོ་སྟེ་རྣམ་པར་ཤེས་པ་དྲུག་པོ་འགགས་མ་ཐག་པ་དེ་ཡིད་ཤེས་སྐྱེད་པའི་དབང་པོ་ཡིན་ནོ།

།ཆོས་ཀྱི་ཁམས་ཞེས་བྱ་བ། ཚོར་བ་འདུ་ཤེས་འདུ་བྱེད་ཀྱི་ཕུང་པོ་གསུམ་དང་། རྣམ་པར་རིག་བྱེད་མིན་པའི་གཟུགས་དང་། འདུས་མ་བྱས་ཐམས་ཅད་དོ།

།འདུས་མ་བྱས་ལ། སོ་སོར་བརྟགས་པས་འགོག་པ་དང་སོ་སོར་བརྟགས་མིན་གྱིས་འགོག་པ་དང་ནམ་མཁའ་དང་གསུམ་དུ་མཛོད་ལས་བཤད། དེ་ལྟ་ན་ཆོས་ཁམས་བདུན་དུ་འདོད། ཡང་སེམས་ཙམ་པ་སོགས་ཀྱིས་དེ་བཞིན་ཉིད་བསྣན་ཏེ་བཞིར་བཞེད།

2
The Elements
Dhatu

[2,1] There are ten elements taken from the aggregate of forms. What are they? 1)-10) They are the five [elements of the sense faculties] from the eye element to the body element and the five [elements of the sense objects] from the element of visible form to the element of textures, thus totaling ten.[10]

[2,2] There are seven elements from the [aggregate of] consciousness: 11)-17) the six from the eye consciousness element to the mind consciousness element, and the mind element, thus totaling seven.

[2,3] The mind element is the mental faculty which is what immediately follows the cessation of [any of] the six [collections of] cognitions. It is the faculty which produces a mental cognition.

[2,4] 18) The element of mental objects are the three aggregates of sensations, perceptions and formations in addition to imperceptible forms and all unconditioned things.

[2,5] Concerning unconditioned things, the three explained in the *Abhidharma Kosha* are cessation due to discrimination, cessation not due to discrimination, and space. In this way there are seven elements of mental objects.

Alternately, the adherents of the Mind Only School hold that there are four [unconditioned things] by adding suchness.

ཀུན་བཏུས་སུ། དགེ་མི་དགེ་ལུང་མ་བསྟན་གྱི་དེ་བཞིན་ཉིད་གསུམ་དང་།
འདུ་ཤེས་མེད་པ་དང་། འགོག་པའི་སྙོམས་འཇུག་གི་དུས་ཀྱི་སེམས་ཁེགས་པའི་གནས་སྐབས་
གཉིས་ཏེ།

གོང་གི་གསུམ་དང་བསྡོམས་པས་འདུས་མ་བྱས་བརྒྱད་དུ་བཞེད་དོ།

།དེ་ལ་སོ་སོར་བརྟགས་འགོག་ནི་སོ་སོར་བརྟགས་པའི་ཤེས་རབ་སོགས་ལམ་གྱི་སྟོབས་ལས་
སྤང་བྱ་ཉོན་མོངས་སོགས་གཏན་དུ་བྲལ་བའི་འདུས་མ་བྱས་ཀྱི་ཆའོ།

།བརྟགས་མིན་འགོག་པ་ནི། སོ་སོར་བརྟགས་པས་ཁེགས་པ་མིན་ཡང་རྒྱུ་རྐྱེན་མ་ཚང་བའི་
སྟོབས་ཀྱིས་གང་ན་གང་མེད་པ་སྟེ་རྟ་ཡི་མགོ་ལ་རྭ་ལྟ་བུའོ།

།ཕྱོགས་གང་ན་བུམ་པ་མེད་པ་ལྟ་བུ་སོགས་མེད་པའི་བྱེ་བྲག་ཐམས་ཅད་འདིར་འདུའོ།

།ནམ་མཁའ་ནི་གཟུགས་རུང་མེད་ཅིང་བྱེད་པ་ཐམས་ཅད་ཀྱི་གོ་འབྱེད་པ་ལ་མི་སྒྲིབ་པའོ།

།དགེ་སོགས་ཆོས་རྣམས་ཀྱི་དེ་བཞིན་ཉིད་ནི་ཆོས་ཀྱི་དབྱིངས་སོ།

།མི་གཡོ་བ་ནི་འདུ་ཤེས་མེད་པའི་སྙོམས་འཇུག་གོ

།འདུ་ཤེས་དང་ཚོར་བ་འགོག་པ་ནི་འགོག་པའི་སྙོམས་འཇུག་གོ

།དེ་ལྟར་ཆོས་ཀྱི་སྐྱེས་མཆེད་པའི་གཟུགས་ལྔ་དང་། ཚོར་འདུ་འདུ་བྱེད་ཀྱི་ཕུང་པོ་གསུམ་དང་།
འདུས་མ་བྱས་བརྒྱད་དེ་བཅུ་དྲུག་པོ་དེ་ལ་ཆོས་ཀྱི་ཁམས་ཞེས་བྱའོ།

According to the *Abhidharma Sammucchaya* it is held that there are:

a) The three [unconditioned things] of the suchness of virtue, [the suchness] of nonvirtue, and [the suchness] of the neutral.

b) The two [unconditioned things] of the occasion of blocked cognition at the time of the serenity of non-perception and of [the serenity of] cessation. Adding these together with the above three, it is held that there are eight unconditioned things.

[2,6] Cessation due to discrimination is the unconditioned quality of being permanently free from what should be relinquished, such as the disturbing emotions, by means of the power of the path, such as discriminating knowledge.

[2,7] Cessation not due to discrimination is not a blocking by means of discrimination. Because of insufficient causes and conditions, it is a nonexistence of something at a certain place, as, for example, horns on the head of a horse. As in the instance of the absence of a vase at a certain location, all kinds of nonexistence are included within this.

[2,8] Space is not capable of being a physical form. It accommodates all activities and it does not obstruct.

[2,9] Suchness of all phenomena such as virtue and so forth is dharmadhatu, the realm of phenomena.

[2,10] The serenity of non-perception is non-transference.

[2,11] The serenity of cessation is the cessation of both perceptions and sensations.

[2,12] The five types of forms that are mental objects, the three aggregates of sensations, perceptions, and formations, and the eight unconditioned things, totaling sixteen, are called elements of mental objects.

[2,13] The three times six elements — from the eye element, [visible] form element, and eye consciousness element to the mind con-

།དེ་ལྟར་མིག་གི་ཁམས་དང་། གཟུགས་ཀྱི་ཁམས་དང་། མིག་ཤེས་ཀྱི་ཁམས་ནས། ཡིད་ཤེས་ཀྱི་བར་དྲུག་ཚན་གསུམ་སྟེ་བཅོ་བརྒྱད་པོ་དེ་ལས། མིག་ནས་ཡིད་ཀྱི་བར་དྲུག་པོ་ཡུལ་ལ་འཛིན་པར་བྱེད་པའི་རྒྱུ་འམ་རིགས་སམ་ས་བོན་གྱི་དོན་དང་། དེ་བཞིན་དུ་གཟུགས་ནས་ཆོས་ཀྱི་བར་དྲུག་པོ་གཟུང་བའི་དང་། མིག་ཤེས་ནས་ཡིད་ཤེས་ཀྱི་བར་དྲུག་པོ་ཡུལ་དངོས་སུ་འཛིན་པའི་རྒྱུ་འམ་རིགས་སམ་ས་བོན་གྱི་དོན་ཏེ་ཁམས་ཞེས་པ་རྒྱུ་འམ་རིགས་དང་ས་བོན་གྱི་དོན་ཅན་ནོ།

།གཞན་ཡང་སྐྱེས་བུ་ཁམས་དྲུག་པ་ཞེས་ས་ཆུ་མེ་རླུང་ནམ་མཁའ་རྣམ་ཤེས་ཀྱི་ཁམས་དྲུག་གསུངས་པ་དེ་ལུས་ཀྱི་འབྱུང་བ་བཞི་དང་། ནང་གི་བུ་ག་སྟོང་པའི་ཆ་ནི་ནམ་མཁའ་དང་། རྣམ་ཤེས་ཀྱི་ཁམས་ཏེ། དེས་མཚོན་པའི་ཁམས་ཀྱི་མིང་གིས་བཏགས་པའི་དབྱེ་བ་གཞན་དག་ཀྱང་དོན་གྱིས་ཁམས་བཅོ་བརྒྱད་དུ་མ་འདུས་པ་མེད་དོ།

།ཁམས་ཀྱི་རབ་དབྱེ་ལ་ཁམས་བཅོ་བརྒྱད་ལས། གཟུགས་ཅན་དུ་གཏོགས་པ་དབང་ལྔ་དོན་ལྔའི་ཁམས་བཅུ་དང་ཆོས་ཁམས་ཀྱི་ཕྱོགས་གཅིག་སྟེ། ལྷག་མ་གཟུགས་ཅན་མིན་པའོ།

།མིག་ལམ་དུ་བསྟན་དུ་ཡོད་པ་ནི་གཟུགས་ཁམས་གཅིག་པུ། ལྷག་མ་བསྟན་མེད་དོ།

།ཕན་ཚུན་ཐོགས་པ་དང་བཅས་པ་ནི་དབང་ལྔ་ཡུལ་ལྔ་སྟེ་གཟུགས་ཅན་བཅུ་ལས་ལྷག་མ་རྣམས་ཐོགས་པ་མེད་པའོ།

།ཟག་མེད་ནི་ཁམས་ཐ་མ་ཡིད་དང་ཡིད་ཤེས་དང་ཆོས་ཁམས་ཀྱི་སེམས་བྱུང་ལམ་བདེན་དུ་གཏོགས་པ་དང་འདུས་མ་བྱས་རྣམས་ཡིན་ལ་དེ་རྣམས་མ་གཏོགས་པའི། ཁམས་ལྷག་མ་རྣམས་ཉོན་མོངས་སྐྱེ་བའི་མངོན་སུམ་གྱི་སྤྱོད་ཡུལ་ཡིན་པའི་ཕྱིར་ཟག་བཅས་སོ།

sciousness element — altogether total eighteen. Among these, the six [elements] from eye to mind have the function of being causes, potentials, or seeds for apprehending an object. Likewise, the six [elements] from [visible] form to mental object have the function of being [causes, potentials or seeds for] the apprehended [object]. And the six [elements] from eye consciousness to mind consciousness have the function of being causes, potentials, or seeds for actual apprehension of an object. Thus element [*dhatu*] means being a cause, a potential, or a seed.

[2,14] Furthermore, the six elements of a person are taught to be the six elements of earth, water, fire, wind, space, and consciousness. These are the four elements of the body and the vacuity of the inner vessels as the space element in addition to the consciousness element.

As indicated by these [six elements], other divisions with the name elements are also essentially all included within the [above] eighteen elements.

[2,15] Among the presentation of eighteen elements, the ones that belong to the category of [elements] having physical form are the ten elements of the five sense faculties and the five sense objects, as well as the one subcategory of the element of mental objects [which is imperceptible forms]. The remaining ones are all without physical form.

[2,16] The [element] that can be demonstrated in the visual field is only the element of [visual] form. The remaining ones cannot be demonstrated.

[2,17] The mutually obstructive [elements] are the ten having physical form: the five sense faculties and the five sense objects. The remaining ones are not obstructible.

[2,18] The undefiling [elements] are the [three] last elements: the mind element, the mind consciousness element, and the mental states of the element of mental objects belonging to the true

།འདོད་པ་ན་ཁམས་ཐམས་ཅད་ཡོད། གཟུགས་ཁམས་ན་དྲི་རོ་དང་སྣ་ལྕེའི་རྣམ་ཤེས་ཀྱི་ཁམས་མ་གཏོགས་པ་བཅུ་བཞི་ཡོད། གཟུགས་མེད་ན་ཁམས་ཐ་མ་གསུམ་གྱི་ཆ་ཤས་ཡོད་དོ།

།སེམས་ཁམས་བདུན་དང་གཟུགས་སྒྲ་དང་ཆོས་ཁམས་བཅུ་ལ་དགེ་མི་དགེ་ལུང་མ་བསྟན་གསུམ་ཆར་ཡོད། ལྷག་མ་རྣམས་ལུང་དུ་མ་བསྟན་པའོ།

།གཟུགས་སྒྲ་དྲི་རོ་རེག་ཆོས་ཀྱི་ཁམས་དྲུག་ཕྱི། ལྷག་མ་བཅུ་གཉིས་ནི་ནང་གིའོ།

།དམིགས་པ་དང་བཅས་པ་ནི་སེམས་ཁམས་བདུན་དང་། ཆོས་ཁམས་ཀྱི་ཕྱོགས་གཅིག་སེམས་བྱུང་རྣམས་སོ། ལྷག་མ་རྣམས་དམིགས་པ་མེད་པའོ།

།རྟོག་བཅས་ནི་ཡིད་དང་ཡིད་ཤེས་ཀྱི་ཆ་དང་ཆོས་ཁམས་ཀྱི་ཕྱོགས་གཅིག་སེམས་བྱུང་གི་ཆ་རྟོག་བཅས་རྣམས་སོ།

།རང་རྒྱུད་ཀྱི་ཚོར་བས་ཟིན་པ་དབང་པོ་ལྔ་དང་ནང་གི་གཟུགས་དྲི་རོ་རེག་དགུའོ།

།ཆོས་ཁམས་ཀྱི་ཕྱོགས་གཅིག་འདུས་མ་བྱས་རྟག་པ་ཡིན་ལ། གཞན་རྣམས་འདུས་བྱས་དང་མི་རྟག་པའོ།

།དབང་པོ་ལྔ་དང་སེམས་སེམས་བྱུང་ནི་འཛིན་པ་དང་། གཞན་རྣམས་གཟུང་བའོ།

paths, in addition to the unconditioned things. The other elements not belonging to these categories are defiling because they are the direct cause for the disturbing emotions to arise.

[2,19] In the Desire Realms, all the [eighteen] elements are present. In the Form Realms there are fourteen [elements], excluding the elements of odor and taste and of the nose and tongue consciousnesses. In the Formless Realms there are the [defiling] aspects of the last three elements.[11]

[2,20] The seven mental elements, visible form and sound, and the elements of mental objects, altogether totaling ten, have the three aspects of being virtuous, unvirtuous, or neutral. All the remaining elements are neutral.

[2,21] Outer elements are the six elements of visible form, sound, odor, taste, texture, and mental object. The remaining twelve are inner elements.

[2,22] The [elements] with focus are the seven mental elements and the part of the element of mental objects which consists of all the mental states. All the remaining ones are without focus.

[2,23] The [elements] with concepts are the subcategory of the mental faculty and the mind consciousness as well as the one aspect of the element of mental objects which is the subcategory of mental states.

[2,24] The nine elements embraced by personal sensation are the five sense faculties and inner form, odor, taste, and textures.

[2,25] One part of the element of mental objects, the unconditioned things, is permanent. All the others are conditioned things and impermanent.

[2,26] The five sense faculties, the consciousnesses [cognitions], and the mental states are what apprehends, whereas all the others are what is apprehended.

།རྟོག་དཔྱོད་གཉིས་དང་བཅས་པ་ནི་རྣམ་ཤེས་ཀྱི་ཁམས་ལྔ་འོ། ཡིད་ཡིད་ཁམས་སེམས་བྱུང་རྣམས་ལ་རྟོག་དཔྱོད་གཉིས་བཅས། གཉིས་མེད། རྟོག་མེད་དཔྱོད་བཅས་གསུམ་ཡོད། དེ་དག་གི་ལྷག་མ་རྣམས་རྟོག་དཔྱོད་མེད་པའོ།

།གཟུགས་ཅན་གྱི་ཁམས་བཅུ་ནི་རྡུལ་ཕྲན་བསགས་པའོ། ལྷག་མ་ནི་མ་བསགས་པའོ།

།གཅོད་བྱེད་ཡིན་པ་དང་བཅད་བྱ་ཡིན་པ་གཟུགས་དྲི་རོ་རེག་བཞི་པོ་ན་སྟེ། སྲེག་འཇལ་ཀྱང་དེ་བཞིན་ནོ།

།གཟུགས་ཅན་བཅུ་དང་མིག་ཤེས་སོགས་ལྔ་ནི་སྒོམ་པས་སྤང་བྱ། ཁམས་ཐ་མ་གསུམ་ལ་མཐོང་སྒོམ་གྱིས་སྤང་བྱ་དང་སྤང་བྱ་མིན་པ་གསུམ་དུ་ཡོད་དོ།

།བྱུང་བ་གསུམ་གྱི་ཁྱད་པར་ཕྱེ་ན། རྣམ་སྨིན་དང་རྒྱས་བྱུང་ནི་ནང་གི་དབང་པོ་ལྔའོ།

།རང་གི་རིགས་འདྲའི་རྒྱུ་མཐུན་དང་རྣམ་སྨིན་ལས་སྐྱེས་པ་སེམས་ཁམས་བདུན་དང་ཆོས་ཁམས་ཀྱི་ཕྱོགས་གཅིག་སེམས་བྱུང་རྣམས་ཏེ་ཐོགས་པ་མེད་པ་བརྒྱད་པོ་དེའི་ཆ་འགའོ།

།སྒྲ་ལ་རྒྱུན་མེད་པས་རྣམ་སྨིན་ལས་སྐྱེས་པ་མིན་ལ། དབྱངས་སྙན་མི་སྙན་དུ་བྱེད་པའི་རྒྱུ་མཐུན་པའི་དབྱིབས་སོགས་རྣམ་སྨིན་ལས་སྐྱེས་པའོ།

།འདི་དག་གི་ལྷག་མ་དབང་པོའི་ཚོགས་པ་ན་ཡོད་པ་རྣམས་ལ་རྒྱུ་མཐུན་རྒྱས་བྱུང་རྣམ་སྨིན་ལས་བྱུང་བ་གསུམ་ཡོད་ལ། ཕྱི་རོལ་གྱི་ཁམས་རྣམས་རྒྱུ་མཐུན་པོ་ན་ལས་སོ།

[2,27] The elements that have both conception and discernment are the five consciousness elements. The elements of the mental faculty and of the mind consciousness as well as all the mental states have three modes: with both conception and discernment, without either, and without conception but with discernment. All the remaining ones have neither conception nor discernment.

[2,28] The ten elements with physical form are agglomerations of particles. The remaining ones are not agglomerations.

[2,29] It is only the four [elements] of form, odor, taste, and texture that can be something that cuts or is cut. The same applies to being burned or weighed.

[2,30] The ten [elements] with form and the five beginning with the eye consciousness are to be discarded by the [path of] cultivation. The three last elements have both aspects [of disturbing emotions] to be discarded and [the undefiling truth of the path] not to be discarded by the [paths] of seeing and cultivation. Thus there are these three modes.

When defining the differences of the [following] three occurrences, the five inner faculties belong to ripening and development. The elements produced from causal resemblance of their own type and from ripening are the seven mental elements, and the one part of the element of mental objects which is the mental states. The [above mentioned] eight [elements] that are not obstructive belong to this subcategory.

Since sound is discontinuous, it is not produced from [karmic] ripening. But, the causes for creating pleasant and unpleasant tones, such as the shape of the throat, are produced from ripening. The remaining ones that are present when the faculties have come together can belong to the three occurrences from causal resemblance, development, or ripening. All the outer elements occur only from causal resemblance.

།རྒྱས་འབྱུང་ཞེས་པ་ལུས་རྒྱས་པའི་རྒྱུ་བཞི་ནི། ཟས་དང་། བསྐུ་མཉེ་དྲིལ་ཕྱིས་སོགས་ལེགས་པར་བྱ་བ་དང་། གཉིད་དང་ཏིང་ངེ་འཛིན་བཞིའོ།

།དབང་པོ་རྣམས་ལ་རང་གི་ཤེས་པ་དངོས་སུ་རྟེན་པའི་བྱ་བ་བྱེད་བཞིན་པ་སད་ཅིང་གཟུགས་ལ་རྟོག་པའི་མིག་དབང་གི་གནས་སྐབས་ལྟ་བུ་ལ་དབང་པོ་རྟེན་བཅས་དང་། དེ་ལྟ་མིན་པ་གཉིད་ལོག་པའི་མིག་དབང་ལྟ་བུ་ལ་དེ་མཚུངས་ཞེས་བྱའོ།

།ཁམས་གོང་མའི་ལུས་ལ་འོག་མའི་མིག་རྟེན་པ་མིན་ཏེ། རང་ས་ན་མིག་མཆོག་ཏུ་གྱུར་པ་ཡོད་པའི་ཕྱིར་རོ།

།ཁམས་འོག་མའི་མིག་དབང་གིས་གོང་མའི་གཟུགས་མི་མཐོང་སྟེ་ཕྲ་བའི་ཕྱིར། རྣ་བའང་དེ་ལྟ་བུའོ། །འདོད་པའི་ཁམས་པས་བསྒོམས་སྟོབས་ཀྱིས་ལྷའི་མིག་རྣ་ཐོབ་ན། བསམ་གཏན་དེ་པའི་སས་བསྡུས་པའི་འབྱུང་བ་རྒྱུར་བྱས་པའི་དབང་པོ་དྭངས་པ་རང་གི་མིག་དང་རྣ་བའི་ཐད་ཀོར་དུ་འབྱུང་སྟེ། དབང་པོ་དེ་ནི་རྟག་ཏུ་རྟེན་བཅས་ཡིན་ལ། ཞར་འོན་ལྟ་བུའི་མ་ཚང་བ་མེད་ཅིང་། ཐག་རིང་བ་དང་ཕྲ་བའི་གཟུགས་དང་། བསྒྲིབ་ཅིང་བར་ཆོད་པ་རྣམས་ཀྱང་མཐོང་བ་དང་ཐོས་པར་བྱེད་པའོ།

།དེ་ཡང་བསམ་གཏན་དང་པོའི་དབང་པོས་རང་ས་དང་འདོད་པའི་སྤྱོད་ཡུལ་ཤེས་པ་སོགས་འགྲེའོ།

།ལྷའི་མིག་དེ་ལྟ་བུ་དགྲ་བཅོམ་པ་ལ་ཡོད་པས་སྟོང་གཉིས་དང་། རང་རྒྱལ་བསེ་རུ་ལྟ་བུས་སྟོང་གསུམ་དང་། སངས་རྒྱས་ཀྱིས་གྲངས་མེད་པའི་བར་དུ་གཟིགས་སོ།

།ལྷའི་མིག་དེ་ཚེ་འདིར་བསམ་གཏན་བསྒོམས་སྟོབས་ཀྱིས་མིན་ཀྱང་། སྔོན་བསྒོམས་པ་སོགས

[2,32] As for development, the four causes for bodily development are 1) food, 2) wholesome activities such as massage, rolling, rubbing etc., 3) sleep, and 4) samadhi.

[2,33] The sense faculties may function as the actual support for their respective consciousnesses: for instance, the occasion of the eye faculty being awake and conceiving a form. This is called faculty with support. On occasion they do not act as supports, as, for example, when the eye faculty has fallen asleep. This is called [faculty] resemblance.

[2,34] The body of the Upper Realms is not a support for the eye of the lower ones because it has the superior eye belonging to its own level. The eye faculty of the realms below does not see the forms of the levels above because they are more subtle. It is in the same way with the ear.

[2,35] A person in the Desire Realms, through the power of meditation, may obtain the divine eye or ear, which consist of subtle faculties made of elements comprised of [the stability in] dhyana that will occur accompanying one's eyes or ears. These faculties are always have a supporting [sense organ] and are without imperfections such as blindness or deafness. The person also sees and hears distant and subtle forms, even those that are covered or obstructed.

[2,36] Moreover, the faculties of the first dhyana perceive the field of experience of their own domain and that of the Desire Realms. It is in the same way with the following [dhyanas].

[2,37] Since, for instance, arhats possess the divine eye, they perceive the secondary thousandfold [universe]. The rhinoceros-like pratyekabuddhas[12] perceive the third thousandfold [universe], and the buddhas perceive countless [universes]. It is taught that this kind of divine eye is not obtained through the power of having practiced the dhyanas within a single lifetime, but occurs from

ཀྱི་རྣམ་སྨིན་ལས་སྐྱེས་པ་སྐྱེ་བས་ཐོབ་པ་ཡོད་ཀྱང་། ངེས་པར་སྲིད་མི་མཐོང་ཞེས་བཤད་དོ། །དེ་ལ་སོགས་པའི་ཁམས་གོང་འོག་གི་དབང་པོ་དང་ཤེས་པ་འབྱུང་ཚུལ་སྣ་ཚོགས་ཤེས་པར་བྱའོ།

།ཁམས་ཀྱི་སྐབས་སོ།

birth and is produced from the ripening of past practice. This divine eye does not perceive the intermediate existence.

[2,38] In this way, it should be understood that there are various kinds of ways in which the faculties and cognitions of the higher and lower realms occur.

[2,39] That was the chapter on the elements.

།སྐྱེ་མཆེད་བཅུ་གཉིས་ནི། མིག་གི་ཁམས་དང་མིག་གི་སྐྱེ་མཆེད་དོན་གཅིག་སྟེ། སོ་སོའི་སྐབས་ཀྱི་རྣམ་བཞག་བྱ་ཚུལ་ཙམ་མོ། དེ་བཞིན་དུ་གཟུགས་ཅན་གྱི་ཁམས་བཅུ་ནི་དེ་དེའི་སྐྱེ་མཆེད་དང་། ཆོས་ཁམས་ནི་ཆོས་ཀྱི་སྐྱེ་མཆེད་དོ།

།རྣམ་པར་ཤེས་པའི་ཁམས་བདུན་ནི། ཡིད་ཀྱི་སྐྱེ་མཆེད་དུ་བསྡུས་པའོ། དེ་ལ་མིག་གི་སྐྱེ་མཆེད་དང་། གཟུགས་ཀྱི་སྐྱེ་མཆེད་ནས། ཡིད་དང་ཆོས་ཀྱི་སྐྱེ་མཆེད་བར་བཅུ་གཉིས་སོ།

།དེ་ཡང་མིག་ནས་ཡིད་ཀྱི་བར་ནང་གི་དྲུག་པོ་འཛིན་པ་དང་། གཟུགས་ནས་ཆོས་ཀྱི་བར་ཕྱིའི་དྲུག་ནི་གཟུང་བ་སྟེ། གཟུང་འཛིན་གྱི་སྒོ་ནས་རྣམ་ཤེས་ཡུལ་ལ་སྐྱེ་ཞིང་མཆེད་པའི་སྒོར་གྱུར་པས་སྐྱེ་མཆེད་ཅེས་བྱའོ།

།ཕུང་པོ་ལྔས་འདུས་བྱས་ཐམས་ཅད་བསྡུས་ཀྱང་། འདུས་མ་བྱས་མ་བསྡུས་ལ། ཁམས་སྐྱེ་མཆེད་དུ་ནི་བསྡུས་པའི་ཕྱིར་འདི་གཉིས་ཀྱི་ཁོངས་སུ་ཤེས་བྱ་ཐམས་ཅད་འདུའོ།

།གོང་དུ་ཁམས་ཀྱི་རབ་དབྱེ་བཤད་པས་སྐྱེ་མཆེད་ལ་ཡང་དེ་ལྟར་དོན་གྱིས་ཤེས་སོ།

།སྐབས་འདིར་ཡིད་ཆོས་ཀྱི་སྐྱེ་མཆེད་ལས་འཕྲོས་ཏེ་ཐ་སྙད་ཀྱི་རྣམ་བཞག་འགའ་ཞིག་བརྗོད་པ་ལ།

3
THE SENSE SOURCES
AYATANA

[3,1] The eye element and the eye source have the same nature, and are thus merely different systems in different contexts. It is likewise with the sources of each of the ten elements with physical form. The element of mental objects is the mental object source. The seven consciousness elements are included within the mind source. Thus in total there are twelve, from the eye source and [visible] form source to the mind source and mental object source.

[3,2] The inner six [sources] from eye to mind are what apprehend, and the outer six from form to mental object are what is apprehended. They are called sources because they are the medium for a cognition to occur and unfold by means of apprehender and apprehended.

[3,3] Although all conditioned things are included within the five aggregates, the unconditioned things are not included. Since the elements are included within the sources, all objects of knowledge can be included within the categories of these two.

[3,4] As the presentation of elements has been dealt with above, understand that the sources are similarly arranged.

[3,5] At this point I will present some of lists of conventions by further explaining the mind source and the mental object source.

ཡིད་ཀྱིས་ནི་མིག་སོགས་ཀྱི་ཡུལ་གཟུགས་སོགས་ཀྱང་ཤེས། དབང་ལྔ་ཡང་རྣམ་ཤེས་དང་རྗེས་སུ་འབྲོ་ལྡོག་གི་ཚུལ་གྱིས་ཡོད་པར་ཤེས་པས་ཤེས་བྱ་ཐམས་ཅད་ཀྱི་ཡུལ་ཅན་ནོ།

།དེར་མ་ཟད་ནང་དུ་ཤེས་པའི་རྒྱུད་གཅིག་གིས་བསྡུས་ཤིང་རང་རིག་པའི་ཕྱིར། ཡིད་ཤེས་རྟོག་མེད་ཀྱི་ཡུལ་དུ་སྒོ་ལྔའི་ཤེས་པ་དང་། ཡིད་རང་དང་བཅས་པ་ཡང་འགྱུར་པས། ཡིད་ནི་ཆོས་ཀུན་གྱི་ཡུལ་ཅན་ཡིན་ལ། དེའི་ཕྱིར་ཡིད་རྟོག་བཅས་ཀྱིས་ནི་ཕྱི་དང་ནང་གི་ཆོས་སོ་ཅོག་ལ་ཐ་སྙད་བྱེད་དུ་རུང་ཞིང་། དེའི་སྒོ་ནས་ཤེས་བྱ་རྣམས་ལ་མ་རྨོངས་པར་འགྱུར་རོ།

།དེས་ན་ཡིད་ནི་ཆོས་ཀུན་གྱི་ཡུལ་ཅན་དང་། ཆོས་རྣམས་ཀྱི་དོན་ཤེས་པར་བྱེད་པ་དང་། འཇུག་ལྡོག་བྱེད་པ་པོ་ཡིན་ལ། ཡིད་དེ་དགེ་ན་ཤེས་པ་གཞན་ཡང་དགེ་བ་སོགས་དང་། ཡིད་དེའི་ཡིད་བྱེད་ཀྱི་དབང་གིས་ཤེས་པ་གཞན་ཡུལ་ལར་ཇུག་ལྡོག་བྱེད་པ་སོགས་ཀྱི་ཕྱིར་ཡིད་ནི་གཙོ་བོ་ཡིན་ཏེ། བཅོམ་ལྡན་འདས་ཀྱིས་མདོ་ལས།

ཆོས་ཀྱི་སྔོན་དུ་ཡིད་འགྲོ་སྟེ། ཡིད་མགྱོགས་ཡིད་ནི་གཙོ་བོ་ཡིན། །ཞེས་གསུངས་པ་ལྟར་རོ།

།དེའི་ཕྱིར་ཤེས་བྱེད་ཐམས་ཅད་བློ་དང་། ཤེས་བྱ་ཐམས་ཅད་ཆོས་སུ་འདུའོ།

།བློ་དེ་ལ་སྒོ་ལྔའི་རྣམ་ཤེས་ནི་རྣམ་པ་ཀུན་ཏུ་རྟོག་མེད་ཡིན་ལ། ཡིད་ལ་རྟོག་བཅས་རྟོག་མེད་གཉིས་ཡོད་དེ།

རྟོག་མེད་ཀྱི་ཤེས་པའི་ཡུལ་ནི། ཡུལ་དུས་རྣམ་པ་མ་འདྲེས་པ། རང་དུས་ཀྱི་རང་མཚན་མིང་གི་སྒྲ་དང་འདྲེས་སུ་མི་རུང་བའོ།

[3,6] Mind cognizes the object of the eye and as well as of the other faculties, which are visible form and the other [sense-objects]. Because it perceives in the manner of engagement [in] and disengagement [from sense-objects] together with the cognitions of [each of] the five sense faculties, it is the perceiver-subject of all knowable things.

[3,7] Moreover, mind consists of a single continuity of cognitive acts within and is individually self-knowing. Mental cognition without concepts therefore has as object the five sense consciousnesses as well as mind itself. Hence mind is the perceiver-subject of all phenomena. Mind with concepts is therefore able to name all outer and inner phenomena, through which it becomes undeluded concerning these objects of knowledge.

[3,8] For this reason, mind is the perceiver-subject of all phenomena. It is also that which makes known the identity of all phenomena, and that which makes the engagement in and the disengagement from [an object or an act]. When the [primary] mind is virtuous, the other cognitions [or consciousnesses] will also be virtuous. Through the power of the activities of this [primary] mind, the other consciousnesses will engage in or disengage from their objects. Mind is therefore the chief factor.

[3,9] This is stated by the Bhagavan [Shakyamuni] in a sutra:

Mind goes before phenomena, mind is swift, mind is the chief.

[3,10] For this reason, all cognitive acts are included within mind and all objects of knowledge within phenomena.

[3,11] Concerning cognition [*blo*], the cognitions of the five sense doors are always nonconceptual, while mental cognition has the two modes of being conceptual and nonconceptual.

[3,12] The object of nonconceptual [mental] cognition is not associated with place, time, and kind. It is never liable to be associated with the sound of its name as the individual characteristic of [the object at] its specific moment.

།རྟོག་བཅས་ཀྱི་ཡུལ་ནི་བུམ་པ་སོགས་ཆོས་རྣམས་ཀྱི་རང་རང་གི་དོན་གྱི་སྤྱི་ཙམ་ཞིག་ཡིད་ངོར་སྣང་བ་སྟེ། འདི་ནི་མིང་གི་སྒྲ་དང་འབྲེལ་སུ་རུང་བ་ཡིན་པས་འདི་ལ་དོན་སྤྱི་འམ་སྒྲ་དོན་ཞེས་བྱ་སྟེ།

བརྡ་ལ་བྱང་བ་རྣམས་ཀྱིས་དེ་དང་སྒྲ་བསྲེས་ནས་བཟུང་བ་དེའི་སྒོ་ནས་ཡུལ་དུས་རྣམ་པ་བསྲེས་པའི་ཚུལ་གྱིས་བུམ་པ་ལ་སོགས་པ་ཆོས་རྣམས་ཀྱི་རྣམ་བཞག་སྣ་ཚོགས་བྱེད་དོ།

།ཞེས་བྱ་དང་། དེའི་དབྱེ་བ་དངོས་དངོས་མེད་གཉིས་དང་། དངོས་པོ་ལ་བེམ་ཤེས་ལྡན་མིན་འདུ་བྱེད་གསུམ་དུ་དབྱེ་བ་ལྟ་བུའི་ཐ་སྙད་དང་། དེ་དག་གོང་མ་གོང་མར་བསྡུ་བ་དང་། ཞེས་བྱ་དང་དངོས་པོ་ནི་བེམ་པོ་སོགས་ཀྱི་སྤྱི་ཡིན་པ་དང་། བེམ་པོ་སོགས་དེའི་བྱེ་བྲག་ཡིན་པ་དང་།

བཏགས་པ་ལ་མི་ལྟོས་པར་རང་ཉིད་རྫས་སུ་ཡོད་པ་སྔོན་པོ་ལྟ་བུ་དང་། བཏགས་པ་ཙམ་གྱིས་ཡོད་པ་སྤྱི་ལ་སོགས་པ་ལྟ་བུ་དང་།

རྟོག་མེད་ཤེས་པ་རྣམས་སྣང་པའི་སྒོ་ནས་རྫས་ལ་འཇུག་པ་དང་། རྟོག་བཅས་ཀྱིས་དེ་མིན་གཞན་རྣམ་པར་བསལ་བས། གཞན་སེལ་ལམ། རྣམ་བཅད་དམ། གཞན་ལས་ལྡོག་པའི་སྒོ་ནས་བཏགས་པ་རྣམས་ལ་སེལ་བས་འཇུག་པ་ཡིན་ཞིང་། དེ་འདྲའི་བཏགས་པ་དེ་ལ་ལྡོག་པ་ཞེས་བྱའོ།

།གཞན་སེལ་དེ་ལ་དོན་རང་མཚན་དེ་གཞན་ལས་ལོག་པའི་ངོ་བོར་གནས་པའི་ཆ་ནས་དོན་རང་མཚན་གྱི་གཞན་སེལ་དང་། གཞན་སེལ་བ་དང་མཐུན་པར་འཛིན་པའི་བློ་ཡི་གཞན་སེལ་གཉིས་ཡོད་དོ།

[3,13] The object of conceptual [mental] cognition is the appearance in the mental field of a mere general object-image or of its attributes, such as a round vase for instance. This [object-image] is [always] liable to be associated with the sound of its name, so it is called object-image or sound-object.

[3,14] Someone accustomed to a name associates [the mental image] with the sound [of its name] and apprehends it. Through the manner of associating place, time, and kind, such a person creates all kinds of categories of phenomena, such as 'vase', for instance.

[3,15] There are names of categories, such as knowables and its subdivisions: [concrete, functional] things and [inconcrete, nonfunctional] non-things. [Functional] things have three subdivisions: matter, mind, and nonconcurrent formations. Each of these [three] are included within the [category] above.

[3,16] Knowables and things are generalities of matter and so forth. Matter and so forth are instances of the [ones above].

[3,17] There are [phenomena with individual characteristics] which have substantial existence without relying on imputation, such as [the color] blue, and [phenomena] which exist merely by imputation, such as a generality.

[3,18] A nonconceptual cognition perceives a substantial thing by means of an appearance. A conceptual [cognition perceives] through excluding other things which are not that [object]. So it is a perception through exclusion of all imputations by means of other-exclusion or elimination, or through being opposed to other things. Because of such [exclusion], imputations are called oppositions [isolates].

[3,19] Other-exclusion has two types. The aspect of the specifically defined object present as the identity which is different from other things is called the other-exclusion of the specifically defined object. Apprehension in accordance with that other-exclusion is called mental other-exclusion.

།སེལ་བ་འཐམ་རྣམ་བཅད་དེའི་སྟོབས་ཀྱིས། གཞན་བུམ་པ་མིན་པ་རྣམ་པར་བཅད་ན། བུམ་པ་རང་ཉིད་ཡོངས་གཅོད་དུ་གྲུབ་ཅིང་།

བུམ་པའི་སྟེང་ན་མ་བྱས་པ་ལས་ལོག་པའི་ཆ་ནས་བྱས་པ། རྟག་པ་ལས་ལོག་པའི་ཆ་ནས་མི་རྟག་པ་སོགས་ལྡོག་པའི་ཆོས་དུ་མར་འབྱེད་པའི་རྣམ་བཞག་བྱེད་དོ།

།ཡང་ཡུལ་ཅན་བློ་ལ་རིགས་བཞི་སྟེ། མ་རྟོགས། ལོག་རྟོག། ཐེ་ཚོམ། ཡང་དག་པར་རྟོགས་པའོ།

མ་རྟོགས་པའི་བྱེ་བྲག་ལ། མངོན་སུམ་སྣང་ལ་མ་ངེས་པ་དང་། རྗེས་དཔག་ཚད་མ་ལ་མ་བརྟེན་པའི་ཡིད་དཔྱོད་གཉིས་ནི། ཡིད་ཤེས་ལ་ངེས་པ་འདྲེན་མི་ནུས་པའི་ཆ་ནས་བཞག་པའོ།

།ལོག་རྟོག་ནི་ཕྱིན་ཅི་ལོག་ཏུ་འཛིན་པའོ། །ཐེ་ཚོམ་ནི་རྩེ་གཉིས་སུ་འཇུག་པ་ཕྱོགས་མ་ཆོད་པའོ།

།ཡང་དག་པར་རྟོགས་པ་ལ་ཀྱུ་མངོན་སུམ་ཚད་མ་དང་། རྗེས་དཔག་ཚད་མ་གཉིས་སོ།

།དེ་གཉིས་ཀྱི་འབྲས་བུ་བཅད་ཤེས་ཏེ་ངེས་ཤེས་སོ།

།ཡུལ་ལ་སྣང་ཡུལ་ནི་རྟོག་མེད་ཤེས་པའི་ཡུལ་གཟུགས་སོགས་ལྟ་བུ།

ཞེན་ཡུལ་ནི་རྟོག་བཅས་ཀྱི་ཤེས་པས་དོན་སྤྱི་ལ་ཡུལ་དུ་ཞེན་པ།

དེ་གཉིས་ཀར་ཡང་སྐྱེས་བུའི་འཇུག་ལྡོག་གི་ཡུལ་དུ་བྱེད་པའི་ཆ་ནས་འཇུག་ཡུལ།

བློས་གཟུང་བར་བྱ་བའི་ཡུལ་ཡིན་པའི་ཆ་ནས་གཟུང་ཡུལ་ཞེས་བརྗོད་ལ།

དེ་ལྟར་ཡུལ་ཡུལ་ཅན་གྱི་རྣམ་བཞག་དང་།

[3,20] By the power of this other-exclusion or elimination, other things which are not a vase are eliminated and the vase itself is exclusively established [selected].

[3,21] There are numerous categories of distinguishing qualities of oppositions such as "made" from the aspect of the vase itself being opposite of "unmade", and "impermanent" from its being opposite of "permanent."

[3,22] The subject, cognition [*blo*], has four types: lack of understanding, misunderstanding, doubting, and correct understanding.

[3,23] Lack of understanding is of two kinds: direct perception without ascertainment, and assumption not supported by valid inference. These two are defined as [lack of understanding] because they are unable to bring certainty to a mental cognition.

Misunderstanding is to apprehend incorrectly. Doubting is to be of two minds, to be indecisive. Correct understanding has two types of cause: valid direct perception and valid inference. Their effect is decisiveness, certain knowledge.

[3,24] Objects are of the following types:

1) An apparent object is an object of nonconceptual cognition, such as a visible form.

2) A taken [determined] object is the conceptual cognition taking hold of the object-image as being an object.

3) In the case of both of these, the term "engaged object" means the object engaged in and disengaged from by a person.

4) The aspect of being an object apprehended by a [conceptual] cognition is called the apprehended object.

[3,25] These were the presentations of subject and object.

[3,26] For the presentations of opposed and related things, there are, [first], two types of opposition.

ཡང་འགལ་འབྲེལ་གྱི་རྣམ་བཞག་ལ། འགལ་བ་གཉིས་ཏེ་རྒྱུན་ནུས་མཚུངས་སུ་མི་འགྲོགས་པ་ལྷན་ཅིག་མི་གནས་འགལ་ཡིན་ལ། དེ་ལ་བདག་འཛིན་དང་བདག་མེད་འཛིན་པ་ལྟ་བུ་བློ་འགལ་དང༌། ཚ་རེག་གྲང་རེག་ལྟ་བུ་དོན་འགལ་དང་གཉིས་ཡོད། ཕན་ཚུན་སྤང་འགལ་ལ་དངོས་འགལ་རྟག་མི་རྟག་ལྟ་བུ། བརྒྱུད་འགལ་འགལ་ཟླའི་ཁྱབ་བྱ་དང་འགལ་ཟླ་ཅིག་ཤོས་ཏེ། རྟག་པ་དང་བྱས་པ་ལྟ་བུ་གཉིས་སོ།

།འབྲེལ་བ་ལ་བྱས་མི་རྟག་ལྟ་བུ་ལྡོག་པ་ཐ་དད་ཀྱང་བུམ་པའི་ཆོས་སུ་ངོ་བོ་ཐ་དད་མེད་པ་ལྟ་བུ་བདག་གཅིག་འབྲེལ། མེ་དུ་ལྟ་བུ་དེ་བྱུང་འབྲེལ་གཉིས་སུ་ཡོད་དོ།

།ཡང་བུམ་པ་ཞེས་པའི་བརྡ་དོན་ལྟོ་ལྡིར་བ་བུམ་པ་འཛོག་བྱེད་ཀྱི་མཚན་ཉིད། དེས་བཞག་པའི་བུམ་པའི་ཐ་སྙད་མཚོན་བྱ། དེ་གཉིས་གང་ལ་སྦྱར་བའི་གཞིར་མཚོན་བྱའི་བྱེ་བྲག་ལས་གསེར་གྱི་ལྟོ་ལྡིར་བའི་གོང་བུ་འཛིན་པ་མཚན་གཞི་ལྟ་བུ་སྟེ། དེ་ལྟར་མཚན་མཚོན་གཞི་གསུམ་གྱི་རྣམ་བཞག་དང༌། ཡང་བུམ་པ་ལྟ་བུ་ཁྱད་གཞི་ཆོས་ཅན་དང༌། དེའི་སྟེང་དུ་ཁ་ཁྱེར་དང་ལྟོ་བ་འདབ་མ་སོགས་དང་བྱས་མི་རྟག་སོགས་ཆོས་ཇི་སྙེད་ཡོད་པ་ཁྱད་པར་གྱི་ཆོས་ཞེས་བྱ་བའི་རྣམ་བཞག་དང༌།

ཡང་བརྗོད་བྱ་རྗོད་བྱེད་ཀྱི་རྣམ་བཞག་ནི། བརྟག་བྱ་ཕྱི་རོལ་གྱི་དོན་དང༌། དེའི་དོན་སྤྱི་བློ་ལ་སྣང་བའི་སྣང་བཏགས་གཅིག་ཏུ་བསྲེས་ནས་བརྡའ་རྣམས་དོན་ལ་འཁྲུལ་བར་འགྱུར་ལ།

དེ་ལ་དཔྱད་ན་མིང་གི་སྒྲས་དངོས་ཀྱི་བརྗོད་བྱ་དོན་སྤྱི། ཞེན་པས་བརྗོད་བྱ་དོན་རང་མཚན། དངོས་ཀྱི་རྗོད་བྱེད་སྒྲ་སྤྱི། ཞེན་པས་རྗོད་བྱེད་སྒྲ་རང་མཚན་ཡིན་ཀྱང༌། ཡིད་རྟོག་བཅས་ཀྱིས་སྒྲ་དང་སྒྲ་སྤྱི་གཅིག་ཏུ་བསྲེས་ཏེ་རྗོད་བྱེད་དང༌། དོན་དང་དོན་སྤྱི་གཅིག་ཏུ་བསྲེས་ཏེ་བརྗོད་བྱར་བཟུང་ནས། རྗོད་བྱེད་ཀྱི་ཚིག་ལས་བརྗོད་བྱའི་དོན་རྟོགས་པ་ཡིན་ནོ།

1) Non-coexistent opposition means that continuity and function do not accompany each other. It has two kinds: mental opposition, such as holding [the notion of] a self and of no self, and factual opposition, such as hot and cold sensations.

2) Mutually exclusive opposition has two kinds: direct opposition, as, for instance, being permanent and impermanent; and indirect opposition, such as being permanent and made.

[3,27] There are two types of relationship. The [first] is same entity relationship, as, for instance, made and impermanent, which although they have different opposites, don't have a different nature in regard to the qualities of a pot, for example. [Secondly] there is resultant relationship, such as fire and smoke.

[3,28] There is, moreover, the triple system of definition, the defined, and the basis for defining. When defining a vase, the definition is a spherical central portion, which is the attribute for labeling it vase. The defined is the name of the vase. And the basis for defining is the basis for establishing the above two, on which is retained the specific attribute of what is characterized: the spherical hollow form [made] of gold.

[3,29] There is also the system, as in the instance of a vase, of the basis of specifics possessing the attributes. These include the so-called specific attributes, all the existing attributes such as snout, belly, petals, being made, and being impermanent.

[3,30] There is, furthermore, the system of the described [meaning] and the describing [word].

[3,31] All names are associates with their objects by mingling the examined, the external object, with its object-image, the perception appearing to the mind, as one single label. When examining this, the object-image directly described by means of the sound of its name is, by apprehending it, the actual described object, and the sound-image directly describing it, is, by apprehending it, the actual describing sound. However, the conceptual mind appre-

དེ་ལ་སོགས་པའི་ཐ་སྙད་དོན་མཐུན་གྱི་རྣམ་བཞག་འདི་དག་ལ་བརྟེན་ནས་ཤེས་བྱའི་དོན་ལ་མ་རྨོངས་པར་འགྱུར་བ་ཡིན་ནོ།

།ཐ་སྙད་དེ་ལ་ཤེས་བརྗོད་འཇུག་གསུམ་དུ་བཞག་པ་ནི་སེམས་དང་ངག་དང་ལུས་ཀྱི་སྒོ་ནས་སོ།

།ཐ་སྙད་བྱེད་པའི་རྒྱུའི་སྒོ་ནས་དབང་ཤེས་ཀྱིས་མངོན་སུམ་མཐོང་ནས་ཐ་སྙད་བྱེད་པ་མཐོང་བའི་ཐ་སྙད། དེ་བཞིན་དུ་ཡིད་ཆེས་པའི་ཚིག་ལས་ཐོས་པ་དང་། རང་གི་ཡིད་ཀྱིས་དཔྱད་ནས་བྱེ་བྲག་ཕྱེད་པ་དང་། རང་རིག་པས་ཉམས་སུ་མྱོང་བ་ལས་ཐ་སྙད་བྱེད་པའི་ཚུལ་བཞི་དང་།

ཡང་ཡིན་ཡོད་དུ་སྒྲུབ་པ་དང་། མེད་མ་ཡིན་དུ་དགག་པ་སྟེ། སྒྲུབ་ཚུལ་གྱི་ཐ་སྙད་དགག་སྒྲུབ་ཀྱི་ཡན་ལག་བཞིའོ། འདི་ནམས་ཀྱིས་མཚོན་ནས་ཐ་སྙད་ཀྱི་ནམ་བཞག་ཁོང་དུ་ཆུད་པར་བྱའོ།

དེ་ལྟར་ཕུང་ཁམས་སྐྱེ་མཆེད་ཀྱི་རྣམ་བཞག་དེ་ཡང་། གཟུགས་ཀྱི་ཕུང་པོ་ནི་སྐྱེ་མཆེད་དང་ཁམས་བཅུ་དང་། ཆོས་ཀྱི་ཁམས་དང་སྐྱེ་མཆེད་ཀྱི་ཕྱོགས་གཅིག་གིས་བསྡུས་སོ།

།དེའི་ཕྱིར་ཆོས་ཀྱི་སྐྱེ་མཆེད་པའི་གཟུགས་འདི་ཕུང་ལྔའི་ནང་ཚན་གྱི་གཟུགས་སུ་བརྗོད་ཀྱི་ཡུལ་ལྔའི་ནང་ཚན་གྱི་གཟུགས་ཁོ་ན་མིན་ནོ།

གཟུགས་བརྙན་དང་སྒྲ་བརྙན་ལྟ་བུ་མིག་རྣའི་ཤེས་པའི་ཡུལ་ཙམ་མིན་པར་ཐ་སྙད་དུ་ཁས་ལེན་པ་ལ་འགལ་བ་མེད་ཀྱང་། དེ་དག་ལ་གཟུགས་སྒྲ་རང་མཚན་པ་གང་ཡང་མེད་པས་མེད་པ་གསལ་སྣང་ཙམ་སྟེ་ཆོས་ཀྱི་སྐྱེ་མཆེད་ཀྱི་གཟུགས་སུ་བསྡུ་ཡི། གཟུགས་སྒྲའི་སྐྱེ་མཆེད་དུ་མི་བསྡུའོ།

hends the combined sound and sound-image as the description, and, apprehends the combined object and object-image as being the described [object]. Described objects are then understood from the describing words.

[3,32] By means of such similar systems of names, one becomes unmistaken about the meaning of knowable objects.

[3,33] Names are defined as known, described or enacted in terms of mind, speech, and body.

[3,34] In terms of the cause for making names, to make a name from the direct perception by means of a sense consciousness is called names made of things seen.

[3,35] Similarly, there are names made of things heard about through trustworthy words, names made of things discerned by examining with one's own mind, and names made of things by means of experiencing through self-knowing. Thus there are four ways [of making names].

[3,36] Moreover, there are the names of the ways of establishing: the four aspects of refuting and establishing, establishing as an identity or as a presence, and refuting as an identity or as an absence.

[3,37] As represented by these, one can understand the various kinds of names.

[3,38] Concerning these presentations of the aggregates, elements, and sources, the form aggregate consists of the ten elements and sources and the one subcategory of the mental object element and source [of mental objects]. The forms that are mental objects are therefore said to belong under the form [aggregate] among the five aggregates, and not only under the [visible] forms among the five [sense] objects.

[3,38] There is no conflict in provisionally claiming that a reflection or an echo is merely the object of the eye or ear consciousness. But since these [phenomena] do not have any intrinsically existent visible form or sound, they are merely a nonexistent vivid

ཡུལ་ལྔའི་བྱེ་བྲག་ཏུ་གྱུར་པའི་གཟུགས་ལ། བསྟན་ཡོད་ཐོགས་བཅས་ནི་ཀ་བུམ་སོགས་ཀྱི་གཟུགས་ལྟ་བུའོ།

།བསྟན་མེད་ཐོགས་བཅས་ནི་དབང་རྟེན་མིག་སོགས་མཐོང་བྱ་འདིའི་ནང་ན་ཤིན་ཏུ་དྭངས་པ་ཉི་འོད་ལྟར་ཡོད་པ་ཕལ་པའི་དབང་པོས་གཟུང་དུ་མེད་ཀྱང་ཐོགས་བཅས་སུ་འདོད་དོ།

།བསྟན་མེད་ཐོགས་མེད་ནི་རྣམ་པར་རིག་བྱེད་མིན་པའི་གཟུགས་ཏེ་དེ་གསུམ་ཙམ་གསུངས་ཀྱང་། གཟུགས་བརྙན་ལ་བསྟན་ཡོད་ཐོགས་མེད་ཀྱི་གཟུགས་ཀྱི་ཐ་སྙད་ཙམ་འདོགས་རུང་བར་མངོན་ནོ།

།རྣམ་པར་ཤེས་པའི་ཕུང་པོ་ནི་ཡིད་ཀྱི་སྐྱེ་མཆེད་དང་ཤེས་པའི་ཁམས་བདུན་གྱིས་བསྡུས་སོ།

།ཕུང་པོ་གཞན་གསུམ་དང་། གཟུགས་ཕུང་གི་ཕྱོགས་གཅིག་ཆོས་ཀྱི་སྐྱེ་མཆེད་ཀྱི་གཟུགས་དང་། འདུས་མ་བྱས་དང་བཅས་པ་ནི་ཆོས་ཀྱི་སྐྱེ་མཆེད་དང་ཆོས་ཀྱི་ཁམས་ཀྱིས་བསྡུས་སོ།

།དེ་ཐམས་ཅད་གཟུགས་ཀྱི་ཕུང་པོ་དང་། ཡིད་ཀྱི་སྐྱེ་མཆེད་དང་། ཆོས་ཀྱི་ཁམས་གསུམ་གྱི་ནང་དུ་འདུའོ།

།ཡང་ཞེས་བྱ་གཞི་ལྔར་འདུ་སྟེ། སྣང་བ་གཟུགས་ཀྱི་གཞི་ནི། གཟུགས་ཀྱི་ཕུང་པོ་སྔར་ཇི་སྐད་བཤད་པ་བཞིན་ནོ།

།གཙོ་བོ་སེམས་ཀྱི་གཞི་ནི། རྣམ་པར་ཤེས་པ་ཚོགས་དྲུག་གམ་བརྒྱད་པོ་དེའོ།

presence, and are thus included under forms that are mental objects rather than under the visible form and sound sources.

[3,39] Form, which is one subcategory of the five aggregates, can be of three types:

a) Visible and obstructive, as, for instance, the form of a pillar or a vase.

b) Invisible and obstructive, such as the sense faculties which are found in very subtle form, similar to sunlight, within the visible sense organs, the eyes and so forth. They cannot be perceived by the sense faculties of ordinary people, yet they are considered to be obstructive.

c) Invisible and non-obstructive [forms] are the imperceptible forms.

While only these three have been traditionally taught, it is evident that a reflected image can be named as visible and non-obstructive form.

[3,40] The consciousness aggregate consists of seven categories: the mind source and the [six] consciousness elements.

[3,41] The other three aggregates and the one subcategory of the form aggregate, the [five] forms that are mental objects, as well as the unconditioned things, are all included under the mental object sources and mental object elements.

[3,42] All of these [above] are included within three [categories]: the form aggregate, the mind source, and the mental object element.

[3,43] Also, they can be contained within the five bases of knowables:

a) The form base of appearance is exactly what was previously explained as the form aggregate.

b) The chief mind base is the six or eight collections of consciousnesses [cognitions].

།འཁོར་སེམས་བྱུང་གི་གཞི་ནི་སེམས་བྱུང་རྣམས་ཏེ་ཚོར་བ་དང་འདུ་ཤེས་དང་བཅས་པའི་སེམས་བྱུང་ང་གཅིག་གོ།

།ལྡན་མིན་འདུ་བྱེད་ནི་སྔར་བཤད་པ་བཞིན་དང་། འདུས་མ་བྱས་ཀྱི་གཞི་ནི་ཆོས་ཀྱི་ཁམས་སུ་སྔར་བཤད་པ་བཞིན་དུ་ཤེས་པར་བྱའོ།

།སྐྱེ་མཆེད་ཀྱི་སྐབས་སོ།

c) The accompanying base of mental states is all the mental states; the fifty-one mental states including sensation and perception.

d) The nonconcurrent formation [base] is as previously explained.

e) The base of unconditioned things should be understood as was previously explained under the mental object elements.

[3,44] This was the chapter on the sources.

།རྟེན་ཅིང་འབྲེལ་བར་འབྱུང་བ་གང་ཞེ་ན།

ཕྱི་དང་ནང་གིས་བསྡུས་པའི་ཆོས་འདི་རྣམས་རྒྱུ་མེད་པར་བྱུང་བ་མ་ཡིན། རྒྱུ་མིན་པ་བདག་དང་དུས་དང་དབང་ཕྱུག་སོགས་བྱེད་པོ་རྟག་པ་གཞན་གྱི་རྒྱུ་ལས་བྱུང་བ་མ་ཡིན་ལ། རང་རང་གི་རྒྱུ་རྐྱེན་རྟེན་འབྲེལ་ཚོགས་པ་ལ་བརྟེན་ནས་སྐྱེ་བ་ནི་རྟེན་ཅིང་འབྲེལ་བར་འབྱུང་བ་ཞེས་བྱ་སྟེ། ཚུལ་འདི་ལྟ་བུར་སྨྲ་བ་ནི་སངས་རྒྱས་ཀྱི་གསུང་ཐུན་མོང་མིན་པའི་རང་ལུགས་སོ།

།དེ་ལ་ཕྱིའི་ཆོས་ཐམས་ཅད་ནི་ས་བོན་ལས་མྱུ་གུ་སྐྱེ་བ་ལ་སོགས་པའི་ཚུལ་དུ་རྟེན་ཅིང་འབྲེལ་བར་འབྱུང་ལ། ནང་གི་ཆོས་སེམས་ཅན་མཆོག་དམན་བར་མའི་ཕུང་པོ་ཐམས་ཅད་ནི་རྟེན་འབྲེལ་ཡན་ལག་བཅུ་གཉིས་ཀྱི་ཚུལ་དུ་འབྱུང་ངོ།

།དེ་ཇི་ལྟར་ན་ཕྱིའི་རྟེན་འབྲེལ་ནི། རྒྱུ་དང་འབྲེལ་བ་བདུན་དང་། རྐྱེན་དང་འབྲེལ་བ་དྲུག་གི་ཚུལ་གྱིས་ས་བོན་ལས་མྱུ་གུ་སོགས་འབྱུང་བའི་དཔེས་མཚོན་ནས་ཤེས་པར་བྱ་སྟེ། རྒྱུ་དང་འབྲེལ་བ་ནི། ས་བོན་དང་མྱུ་གུ་དང་། འདབ་མ་དང་། སྡོང་བུ་དང་། སྦུ་གུ་དང་། སྙིང་པོ་དང་། མེ་ཏོག་དང་། འབྲས་བུ་རྣམས་སྔ་མ་ལས་ཕྱི་མ་རིམ་བཞིན་སྐྱེ་བ་ཉེར་ལེན་གྱི་རྒྱུའི་དབང་དུ་བྱས་ཏེ་གསུངས་སོ།

།རྐྱེན་དང་འབྲེལ་བ་ནི། ས་ཆུ་མེ་རླུང་ནམ་མཁའ་དུས་དང་དྲུག་སྟེ། རིམ་པ་ལྟར་བརྟེན་པ་དང་སྡུད་པ་དང་སྨིན་པ་དང་འཕེལ་བ་དང་གོ་འབྱེད་པ་དང་རིམ་པས་འགྱུར་བར་བྱེད་དེ། ལྷན་ཅིག་བྱེད་པའི་རྐྱེན་འདི་དག་གིས་མྱུ་གུ་ནས་འབྲས་བུའི་བར་དུ་བདུན་པོ་འབྱུང་བའི་གྲོགས་བྱེད་དོ།

4
Dependent Origination

[4,1] What is meant by dependent origination? It means that nothing included under inner or outer phenomena has arisen without a cause. They have also not originated from an independent cause, an uncaused and permanent creator such as the Self, Time, or the Almighty. The fact that phenomena are produced based on the interdependence of their respective causes and conditions coming together is called dependent origination. To proclaim this is the unique approach of the Buddha's teaching.

[4,2] All outer phenomena arise in interdependence, in the manner of, for instance, a sprout growing from a seed. Inner phenomena, the aggregates of higher, medium, and lower beings, originate in the manner of the twelve links of interdependence.

[4,3] How is this? The outer interdependence can be illustrated by the example of such things as a sprout growing from a seed, by means of seven related causes and six related conditions.

[4,4] The [seven] related causes are taught to be seed, sprout, stamen, stalk, bud, flower, and fruit, which sequentially are the causes that perpetuate the consecutive origination.

[4,5] The [six] related conditions are earth, water, fire, wind, space, and time, which respectively stabilizes, causes to adhere, matures, expands, accommodates, and gradually changes.

These co-operating conditions assist in the origination of the seven [steps] from sprout to fruit.

།ནང་གི་རྟེན་འབྲེལ་ལ་རྒྱུ་དང་འབྲེལ་བ་ནི་ཡན་ལག་བཅུ་གཉིས་ཏེ། གང་ཞེ་ན་མདོ་ལས། རྟེན་ཅིང་འབྲེལ་བར་འབྱུང་བ་ཞེས་བྱ་བ་ནི་འདི་ལྟ་སྟེ། འདི་ཡོད་པས་ན་འདི་འབྱུང་ལ། འདི་སྐྱེས་པའི་ཕྱིར་འདི་སྐྱེ་བ་སྟེ། གང་འདི་མ་རིག་པའི་རྐྱེན་གྱིས་འདུ་བྱེད་རྣམས། འདུ་བྱེད་ཀྱི་རྐྱེན་གྱིས་རྣམ་པར་ཤེས་པ་སོགས་ནས། དེ་བཞིན་དུ་མིང་དང་གཟུགས་དང་། སྐྱེ་མཆེད་དྲུག། རེག་པ། ཚོར་བ། སྲེད་པ། ལེན་པ། སྲིད་པ། སྐྱེ་བ། རྒ་ཤིའི་བར་དུ་སྨྲས་ཤིང་། མྱ་ངན་དང་། སྨྲེ་སྔགས་འདོན་པ་དང་། སྡུག་བསྔལ་བ་དང་། ཡིད་མི་བདེ་བ་དང་། འཁྲུགས་པ་རྣམས་འབྱུང་སྟེ། དེ་ལྟར་སྡུག་བསྔལ་གྱི་ཕུང་པོ་ཆེན་པོ་འབའ་ཞིག་པོ་འདི་འབྱུང་བར་འགྱུར་རོ།

།དེ་ལ་མ་རིག་པ་འགགས་པས་འདུ་བྱེད་འགགས་སོགས་ནས། སྐྱེ་བ་འགགས་པས་རྒ་ཤི་དང་མྱ་ངན་སོགས་སྡུག་བསྔལ་གྱི་ཕུང་པོ་ཆེན་པོ་འབའ་ཞིག་པོ་འདི་འགག་པར་འགྱུར་རོ། །ཞེས་གསུངས་པ་ལྟར། བདེན་དོན་མི་ཤེས་ཤིང་། ཁམས་གསུམ་གྱི་རང་སའི་ཕུང་པོ་རྣམས་ལ། རྟག་པ་དང་བདེ་བ་དང་བདག་དང་རི་ལ་པོ་དང་གཅིག་པུ་དང་སེམས་ཅན་དང་བདག་གིར་འདུ་ཤེས་པ་ལ་སོགས་པ་དངོས་པོའི་རང་བཞིན་དང་མི་མཐུན་པར་ཕྱིན་ཅི་ལོག་ཏུ་འཛིན་པའི་རྨོངས་པ་ཡང་དག་པའི་དོན་ལ་སྒྲིབ་པར་བྱེད་པའི་ཀུན་རྟོག་དེ་ལ་མ་རིག་པ་ཞེས་བྱའོ།

།བདག་ཏུ་འཛིན་པའི་མ་རིག་པ་དེ་ཡོད་ན་དེའི་དབང་གིས་ཆགས་སྡང་གཏི་མུག་གིས་བསྐྱེད་པའི་ལས་བསོད་ནམས་དགེ་བ་དང་། བསོད་ནམས་མིན་པ་མི་དགེ་བ་དང་། མི་གཡོ་བའི་ལས་རྣམས་འབྱུང་བས་ན། རྣམ་ཤེས་ལ་ཡང་སྲིད་ཀྱི་ས་བོན་འདེབས་པས་འདུ་བྱེད་ཅེས་བྱ་སྟེ། དགེ་བས་མཐོ་རིས་ཀྱི་རྟེན་དང་བདེ་བ། མི་དགེ་བས་ངན་སོང་གི་རྟེན་དང་སྡུག་བསྔལ། མི་གཡོ་བས་ཁམས་གོང་མ་གཉིས་ཀྱི་ཡང་སྲིད་འདུ་བྱེད་དོ།

[4,6] As to inner interdependence, the related causes are the twelve links. What are they? A sutra describes them:

"Dependent origination is as follows: Because this exists, such-and-such will arise. Because that has arisen, such-and-such arises. Hence, because of ignorance the formations arise, because of the formations the consciousnesses will arise, and so forth. The same holds true for name-and-form, the six sense-sources, contact, sensation, craving, grasping, becoming, and birth down to old age and death. Sorrow, lamentation, misery, unhappiness and distress will then arise. Thus this great mass of total suffering arises."

[4,7] "Similarly, the formations will cease because of ignorance having ceased and so forth, down to the point where, because of birth, old age and death having ceased, sorrow and so forth, this great mass of total suffering will also cease." Thus it has been taught.

[4,8] 1) IGNORANCE: Ignorance means not to know the meaning of the [four noble] truths, as well as the delusion of perceiving incorrectly and in disharmony with the nature of things, such as regarding the respective aggregates of the various levels in the three realms as being permanent, pleasant, a self-entity, whole, singular, a sentient being, and 'my,' all of which are conceptualizations that obscure the correct meaning.

[4,9] 2) FORMATION: As long as this ignorance which apprehends a self is present, it results in the power of actions [karmic formations] created by attachment, anger and delusion, the meritorious actions of virtue, the non-meritorious actions of nonvirtue, and the non-transferring actions. Formation therefore means that seeds of reincarnation are being planted in the consciousness. Thus, virtue forms the [bodily] support and pleasures of the higher realms, nonvirtue forms the support and sufferings of the lower realms, and the non-transferring [karma] forms the rebirths in the two upper realms [of form and formlessness].

།འདུ་བྱེད་དེས་ཕྱི་མའི་སྲིད་པའི་སྐྱེ་གནས་སུ་འགྲོ་བའི་རྣམ་ཤེས་འབྱུང་བར་བྱེད་དེ། ཡང་སྲིད་འཕེན་བྱེད་ཀྱི་ས་བོན་རྣམ་ཤེས་ལ་བཞག་པ་འཕེན་བྱེད་ཀྱི་རྣམ་ཤེས་དང་།ནམ་ཞིག་རྐྱེན་ཚོགས་ནས་སྲིད་པའི་སྐྱེ་གནས་སུ་ཁྲིད་པ་འཕངས་འབྲས་ཀྱི་རྣམ་ཤེས་ཞེས་བྱ་ཞིང་། དེ་གཉིས་ཀ་དོན་དུ་ཡང་སྲིད་འགྲུབ་བྱེད་རྣམ་ཤེས་ཀྱི་ཡན་ལག་ཏུ་གཅིག་གོ།

།རྣམ་ཤེས་དེའི་དབང་གིས་མངལ་དུ་ཉིང་མཚམས་སྦྱོར་བ་ན་རྣམ་ཤེས་དང་ཚོར་འདུ་འདུ་བྱེད་དེ་མིང་བཞི་དང་། དེ་དང་ལྷན་ཅིག་པའི་མེར་མེར་པོ་ལ་སོགས་པ་གཟུགས་ཏེ་མིང་གཟུགས་ཀྱི་ཡན་ལག་དེ་དག་མདུང་ཁྲིམ་ལྟར་ཕན་ཚུན་བརྟེན་པའི་ཚུལ་གྱིས་སྲིད་པའི་ལུས་ཀུན་ནས་འཛིན་པ་འབྱུང་ངོ་།

།དེ་ལས་མིང་གཟུགས་ཀྱི་གནས་སྐབས་ཡོངས་སུ་རྫོགས་པ་ནང་གི་མིག་སོགས་སྐྱེ་མཆེད་དྲུག་འབྱུང་ངོ་།

།དེ་ལས་ཡུལ་དབང་ཤེས་གསུམ་འདུས་ནས་ཡུལ་གྱི་འགྱུར་བ་ཡོངས་སུ་གཅོད་པ་མིག་གི་འདུས་ཏེ་རེག་པ་སོགས་དྲུག་འབྱུང་བ་ནི་རེག་པའི་ཡན་ལག་གོ།

།རེག་པ་དེ་ལས་ཚོར་བ་བདེ་སྡུག་བཏང་སྙོམས་གསུམ་གྱི་ཆ་ལ་ཉེ་བར་ལོངས་སྤྱོད་པ་འབྱུང་བ་ནི་ཚོར་བའི་ཡན་ལག་གོ།

།ཚོར་བ་དེ་ལ་བརྟེན་ནས་ཚོར་བ་བདེ་བ་ལ་མི་འབྲལ་བར་འདོད་པའི་འདོད་སྲེད། མི་བདེ་བ་ལ་འདོར་བར་འདོད་པའི་འཇིགས་སྲེད། བཏང་སྙོམས་ལ་རང་གར་གནས་ཤིང་། གཟུགས་ནས་ཆོས་ཀྱི་བར་ཡུལ་དྲུག་པོ་དེ་ལ་སྲེད་པ་སྐྱེ་སྟེ། མདོར་ན་ཚོར་བའི་རྒྱུ་ལས་ཡུལ་གྱི་རོ་མྱང་བ་དང་དགའ་ཞིང་ཞེན་པ་སྐྱེ་བས་ཡུལ་སྡུད་པ་ནི་སྲེད་པའི་ཡན་ལག་གོ།

[4,10] 3) CONSCIOUSNESS: These formations give rise to the consciousness which goes to the birthplace of the next existence. The seed placed in the [all-ground] consciousness which propels one to the [next] rebirth is called impelling consciousness, and that which leads to the birthplace of that life once the conditions have come together is called the consciousness of the impelled result. Both of these are in fact one, in terms of being the link consciousness that establishes a rebirth.

[4,11] 4) NAME-AND-FORM: When by the power of this consciousness one is connected to a womb, the link of name-and-form consists of the four 'names' of consciousness, sensation, perception, and formation, and together with them the form which is the oval fetal form and so forth. These constitute the body of that existence by means of mutually supporting each other, as in the case of the roofbeams of a house.

[4,12] 5) THE SIX SOURCES: Following that, when the period of name-and-form has been fully completed, the inner six sources of the eye and so forth arise.

[4,13] 6) CONTACT: Thereafter the objects, sense faculties and consciousnesses will meet together and the six contacts will arise, such as perception through the contact of the form of an object meeting with the eye. This is the link of contact.

[4,14] 7) SENSATION: From this contact arises the experience of the three aspects of pleasant, painful, and indifferent sensations. That is the link of sensation.

[4,15] 8) CRAVING: Based on sensation arises the eager craving of desiring not to be separated from a pleasant sensation, the fearful craving of desiring to cast away an unpleasant sensation, and a self-sufficient abiding in regards to indifferent sensations. Thus arises a craving towards the six objects, from forms to mental objects. In short, the link of craving is to experience the taste of the objects caused by sensation, and to draw in these objects

།འདི་ལ་འདོད་གཟུགས་གཟུགས་མེད་ཀྱི་སྲིད་པ་གསུམ་སོགས་སུ་དབྱེར་ཡོད་དོ།

།སྲིད་པ་དེ་ལས་བདག་སྡུག་པ་དང་བདེ་བའི་ངོ་བོ་ལས་གྲོལ་བར་མ་གྱུར་ཅིག། ཅེས་བརྐམ་ཆགས་ཀྱི་སྲིད་པ་ལྷག་པར་འཕེལ་ཏེ། ཡུལ་དང་དུ་ལེན་པ་ལ་དངོས་སོ་སྦྱོར་བ་ནི་ལེན་པའི་ཡན་ལག་སྟེ། འདི་ལ་དབྱེ་བ་བྱས་ན། འདོད་པ་དང་ལྟ་བ་དང་ཚུལ་ཁྲིམས་བརྟུལ་ཞུགས་མཆོག་འཛིན་དང་བདག་ཏུ་སྨྲ་བ་ཉེ་བར་ལེན་པ་བཞིར་ཡང་གསུངས་སོ།

།ལེན་པ་དེས་ལུས་ངག་ཡིད་གསུམ་གྱི་སྒོ་ནས་སྲིད་པ་ཕྱི་མ་འགྲུབ་པའི་ལས་མངོན་དུ་བྱས་པ་ནི་སྲིད་པའི་ཡན་ལག་སྟེ་ཁམས་གསུམ་གྱི་སྲིད་པ་གསུམ་སོགས་སུ་དབྱེར་ཡོད་དོ།

།སྲིད་པ་དེའི་མཐུས་ནམ་ཞིག་རྐྱེན་ཚོགས་པ་ན། ཡང་སྲིད་ཀྱི་སྐྱེ་གནས་དེར་དངོས་སུ་དང་པོར་སྐྱེ་བ་དང་ལུས་རྫོགས་པ་དང་རིས་མཐུན་པར་གནས་པ་ནི་སྐྱེ་བའི་ཡན་ལག་སྟེ། དེ་ནི་རྟེན་དེ་ལ་སྡུག་བསྔལ་ཇི་སྙེད་མྱོང་བའི་གཞིར་གྱུར་པ་ཡིན་ནོ།

།སྐྱེ་བ་དེ་ལས་ཕུང་པོའི་རྒྱུན་འགྱུར་པའི་རྒ་བ་དང་། རྒྱུན་འགགས་པའི་ཤི་བ་དང་། དེས་མཚོན་ནས་ནང་གི་ཡོངས་སུ་གདུང་བ་སྨྱུ་ངན་དང་། དེ་ལས་བྱུང་བའི་ཚིག་སྨྲ་བ་སྨྲེ་སྔགས་འདོན་པ། སྒོ་ལྔའི་ཤེས་པ་དང་མཚུངས་ལྡན་གྱི་སྡུག་བསྔལ་བ། ཡིད་ཤེས་དང་མཚུངས་ལྡན་གྱི་ཡིད་མི་བདེ་བ། གཞན་ཡང་ཉམས་སུ་མི་བདེ་བའི་ཉེ་ཉོན་རྣམས་འབྱུང་བ་འཁྲུགས་པ་སྟེ། དེ་ལྟར་མདོར་ན་སྡུག་བསྔལ་གྱི་ཕུང་པོ་ཆེན་པོ་འབའ་ཞིག་པ་འདི་ནི་འཁོར་བར་སྐྱེ་བ་ལས་བྱུང་བའོ།

།སྐྱེ་བ་དེ་ཡང་སྲིད་པ་ལས་བྱུང་བ་སོགས་ཡན་ལག་སྔ་མ་སྔ་མ་འདི་དག་ཡོད་པས་ཕྱི་མ་ཕྱི་མ་དག་ཡོད་པའི་ཐ་སྙད་འབྱུང་ལ། སྔ་མ་དག་སྐྱེས་པས་ཕྱི་མ་སྐྱེ་བའི་དོན་བྱེད་པ་ཡིན་ཞིང་། སྔ་མ་མེད་པ་དང་མ་སྐྱེས་པ་ན་ཕྱི་མ་འདི་མི་འབྱུང་ལ་མི་སྐྱེ་བ་ཡིན་པས། སྡུག་བསྔལ་གྱི་ཕུང་པོ

because of taking delight in clinging to them. It is divided into the three cravings of the realms of Desire, Form and Formlessness.

[4,16] 9) GRASPING: From this craving greatly increases the eager craving of [thinking] "May I not be separated from what is beautiful and pleasant!" Hence the actual involvement in fervently grasping for objects is the link of grasping. When subdivided, it is taught that there are the four types of grasping: of desire, of [wrong] beliefs, of holding discipline and ritual to be paramount, and of adhering to a self.

[4,17] 10) BECOMING: This grasping fully creates the actions through body, speech, and mind that establish the following existence. This is the link of becoming. It can be subdivided into the three types of becoming of the three realms and so forth.

[4,18] 11) REBIRTH: By the power of this becoming, once the conditions have assembled, the link of rebirth is to first actualize the rebirth in the birth place of that reincarnation, to fully develop a body and to remain as one's similar class. It is the basis for experiencing all kinds of suffering through that [bodily] support.

[4,19] 12) OLD AGE AND DEATH: From rebirth comes aging, which is the change in the continuity of the aggregates, and death, which is the ceasing of that continuity. Illustrated thereby, from this arises the sorrow which is inner anguish, the lamentation uttered therefrom, the misery which accompanies the five sense consciousnesses, and the unhappiness which accompanies the mind consciousness. In addition arises distress caused by the unpleasant subsidiary disturbing emotions. In short, this great mass of total suffering results from rebirth within samsara.

[4,20] This rebirth results from becoming and its accompanying [links]. Since the former links exist, there is the convention that the following ones will arise. The former ones, having arisen, will perform the function of making the following links arise. When

འགག་པར་འགྱུར་རོ།

།རྐྱེན་དང་འབྲེལ་བ་ནི་མ་རིག་པ་སོགས་ཉོན་མོངས་རྣམས་དམིགས་པའི་ཡུལ་དང་ནང་གི་དབང་པོ་སོགས་ཀྱིས་ཀུང་གྲོགས་བྱས་ནས་སྐྱེ་ལ། ལས་ཀུང་དེ་བཞིན་ཏེ། སྡུག་བསྔལ་གྱི་གཞི་མིང་གཟུགས་སོགས་བདུན་ནི། ནང་གི་སའི་ཁམས་སྲ་བ་དང་། ཆུ་གཤེར་བདང་། མེ་དྲོ་བས་ཟས་སོགས་འཇུ་བ་དང་། དབུགས་འབྱིན་རྔུབ་སོགས་རླུང་གི་ཁམས་དང་། གོ་འབྱེད་པའི་བུ་ག་རྣམས་ནམ་མཁའི་ཁམས་དང་། རྣམ་པར་ཤེས་པའི་ཁམས་ཏེ་ཁམས་དྲུག་གིས་ལྷན་ཅིག་བྱེད་པའི་རྐྱེན་བྱས་ནས་སྐྱེ་བར་བྱེད་དོ།

།མིག་ཤེས་ནི་རྟེན་མིག་དབང་དང་། དམིགས་པ་གཟུགས་དང་། མངོན་པར་སྣང་བ་དང་། མི་སྒྲིབ་པ་ནམ་མཁའ་དང་། བསམ་པ་ཡིད་བྱེད་ལྷས་ལྷན་ཅིག་བྱས་ནས་སྐྱེ་བ་དེ་བཞིན་དུ་ཤེས་པ་གཞན་ལ་འང་ཅི་རིགས་སུ་སྦྱར་ཏེ་ཤེས་པར་བྱའོ།

།དེ་ལྟར་ཕྱི་དང་ནང་གི་ཆོས་ཐམས་ཅད་རང་རང་གི་རྒྱུ་རྐྱེན་ཅི་ཙམ་ཚོགས་དགོས་པ་ལས་གང་ཡང་རུང་བ་མ་ཚང་ན་མི་སྐྱེ་ལ། ཚང་ན་ངེས་པར་སྐྱེ་བ་རྟེན་ཅིང་འབྲེལ་བར་འབྱུང་བའི་ངང་ཚུལ་ཏེ། ཐོག་མ་མེད་པའི་དུས་ནས་རྒྱུན་གྱི་འཇུག་པ་འདི་ལ་བྱེད་པ་པོ་བདག་དང་དབང་ཕྱུག་སོགས་གང་ཡང་མེད་ལ། རྒྱུ་རྣམས་ཀྱིས་རང་འབྲས་འདི་དག་སྐྱེད་དོ་སྙམ་དུ་མི་རྟོག། འབྲས་བུ་རྣམས་ཀྱིས་བདག་འདིས་སྐྱེད་དོ་སྙམ་དུ་མི་རྟོག་ཀུང་།

རྒྱུ་འབྲས་ཀྱི་རྟེན་འབྲེལ་ཁྱད་པར་ལྔ་ལྡན་དུ་འབྱུང་སྟེ།

གང་ཞེ་ན། ས་བོན་མ་འགགས་པར་ཡོད་བཞིན་མྱུ་གུ་སྐྱེ་བ་མིན་པར་ས་བོན་འགགས་ནས་མྱུ་གུ་སྐྱེ་བའི་ཕྱིར་རྟག་པ་མིན་པ་དང་།

the former links are absent or have not arisen, the following ones will not originate or arise, and so the mass of suffering will cease.

[4,21] As for the related conditions, the disturbing emotions such as ignorance arise with the cooperation of the inner faculties and the objects focused upon. It is the same way with actions [karmas].

[4,22] The seven [links] such as name-and-form which are the basis for suffering arise from the cooperating conditions of the six elements: the inner solid element of earth, the liquid element of water, the warmth of fire through which food is digested, the wind element such as the inhalation and exhalation of breath, the space element which is all the accommodating cavities, and the consciousness element.

[4,23] A visual cognition [eye consciousness] arises when five things operate together: the support which is the eye faculty, the object which is a visible form, its actual presence, unobscured space and an apprehending frame of mind. It should be understood that this is likewise to be combined with any of the other cognitions [consciousnesses].

[4,24] In this way, the arising of all outer and inner phenomena require that their respective causes and conditions come together in the appropriate manner. When these [factors] are incomplete, phenomena do not arise, while when complete, they will definitely arise. That is the nature of dependent origination.

[4,25] Since beginningless time there has been no creator of this continual involvement, such as the Self, the Almighty or others. Also, the causes do not conceive of the thought, "I will produce this effect" and the effects do not conceive the thought, "I was produced from that." Yet, they arise possessing the five special features of interdependence of cause and effect. What are they?

1. [Phenomena are] not permanent, because a sprout arises after the seed has ceased and not while the seed is unceasingly present.

ས་བོན་འགགས་ཏེ་རྐྱེན་ཚང་པ་ལས་སྐྱེ་བ་མིན་པར་ས་བོན་འགག་པ་དང་མྱུ་གུ་སྐྱེ་བ་སྲང་མདའི་མཐོ་དམན་བཞིན་དུ་བར་མ་ཆད་པར་འབྱུང་བས་ཆད་པ་མིན་པ་དང་།

ས་མྱུག་དེ་གཉིས་ངོ་བོ་དང་བྱེད་ལས་ཀྱི་སྒོ་ནས་གཅིག་མིན་པས་སྤོ་མ་ཕྱི་མར་འཕོས་པ་མིན་པ་དང་།

ས་བོན་ཆུང་ངུས་འབྲས་བུ་ཆེ་བ་འབྱིན་པས་རྒྱུ་ཆུང་ངུས་འབྲས་བུ་ཆེན་པོ་འགྲུབ་པ་དང་། གྲོ་ཡི་ས་བོན་ལས་གྲོ་ཡི་མྱུ་གུ་དང་། དགེ་བ་ལས་བདེ་བ་ལྟ་བུ་རྒྱུ་དང་འབྲས་བུ་འདྲ་བའི་རྒྱུད་དམ་རྒྱུ་མཐུན་པ་ལྟ་ཡི་ཚུལ་དུ་ཕྱི་ནང་གི་རྒྱུ་འབྲས་རྣམས་ཤེས་པར་བྱ་སྟེ།

དཔེ་ཇི་ལྟར་ན། ཁ་ཐོན་མར་མེ་མེ་ལོང་རྒྱ། །མེ་ཤེལ་ས་བོན་སྐྱུར་དང་སྒྲས། །ཕུང་པོ་ཉིང་མཚམས་སྦྱོར་བ་ཡང་། །མི་འཕོ་བར་ཡང་མཁས་རྟོགས་བྱ། ཞེས་གསུངས་པ་ལྟར་ཤེས་པར་བྱ་སྟེ།

དེ་ལྟར་རྟོགས་ན་ཆོས་འདི་དག་རྟེན་འབྲེལ་གྱི་སྣང་བ་བསླུ་མེད་ཙམ་ལས། བདག་དང་གཞན་དང་གཉིས་ཀ་དང་རྒྱུ་མེད་ལས་མ་བྱུང་བས་མ་སྐྱེས་པ། དུས་དང་དབང་ཕྱུག་སོགས་བྱེད་པོས་མ་བྱས་པ། སྲོག་དང་གང་ཟག་དང་བྱེད་པ་པོ་དང་བདག་དང་ཆོས་ཀྱི་ངོ་བོ་མེད་པ། གསོག་དང་གསོབ་དང་རང་བཞིན་མེད་པར་ཤེས་ནས། བདག་སྔོན་དང་ད་ལྟ་ཕྱི་མར་ཅི་ལྟར་གྱུར་པའི་མཐའ་ལ་རྟོག་པ་སོགས་ཀྱི་གཡོ་བ་དང་བྲལ་ཏེ་ཕྱིས་མི་སྐྱེ་བར་བྱེད་པའི་བཟོད་པ་དང་ལྡན་པ་དེ་ལ་སངས་རྒྱས་རྣམས་ཀྱིས་བླ་མེད་བྱང་ཆུབ་ཏུ་ལུང་སྟོན་པར་འགྱུར་རོ།

2. [Phenomena are] not interrupted, because a sprout does not arise from the discontinuance, the seed having ceased; it arises uninterruptedly. The cessation of the seed and the arising of the sprout are like the up-and-down movement of the two sides of a set of balances.

3. The former link is not transformed into the following one, because a seed and a sprout are not one, either in terms of identity or of function.

4. A small cause can produce a big effect, just as a tiny seed can yield a big fruit.

5. Cause and effect have similar continuity or basis, since, for instance, a wheat sprout comes from a wheat seed and pleasure results from virtue.

One should understand that all outer and inner causes and effects are characterized by these five [special features].

[4,26] What is an example for this? Here is how it should be understood:

Like a recitation, a butter lamp, a mirror, a stamp,
A magnifying glass, a seed, sourness, or a sound,
So also with the continuation of the aggregates [reincarnation]
Should the wise realize that they do not transmigrate.

[4,27] Realizing this, you understand that all things are merely an unfailing manifestation of interdependence. Because they have not occurred either through themselves, through something other, through both, or without causes, they are therefore unoriginated [nonarising]. They are not made by a creator such as Time or the Almighty. They are devoid of a life principle or a personality, a doer or a self, or the identity of things. They are hollow and false, and are devoid of a self-nature. The one who understands that this is so, is unaffected by [the 360 unwholesome beliefs], such as conceptualizing a self in the past, present or future.

།དེ་ལྟར་རྟེན་འབྲེལ་ཡན་ལག་བཅུ་གཉིས་པོ་ནི་མ་རིག་པ་མ་སྤངས་ཀྱི་བར་དུ་རྒྱུན་གྱིས་འཇུག་སྟེ། སྔོན་གྱི་དུས་ཀྱི་རྒྱུ་མ་རིག་པ་དང་འདུ་བྱེད་ཀྱིས་ནི་ད་ལྟའི་འཕངས་འབྲས་ཀྱི་རྣམ་ཤེས་ནས་ཉོན་མོངས་སྲིད་ལེན་གྱིས་ཡང་སྲིད་འགྲུབ་བྱེད་ཀྱི་ལས་བསགས་པ་སྲིད་པའི་བར་དུ་འབྱུང་ལ། དེ་ལས་སླད་མའི་ཚེ་ལས་དང་མཐུན་པར་གནས་རིས་གང་དུ་སྐྱེ་བ་ལེན་ཅིང་། རྟེན་དེས་འཁོར་བའི་སྡུག་བསྔལ་རྒ་ཤི་སོགས་མྱོང་ངོ་།

།དེ་ལྟར་གྱུར་པའི་རྟེན་དེ་ལ་ཡང་། གཟུགས་ཅན་གྱི་སེམས་ཅན་རྣམས་ལ་རྣམ་ཤེས་ནས་སྲིད་པའི་བར་འབྱུང་ཞིང་། གཟུགས་མེད་དུ་སྐྱེ་བ་ན་རྣམ་ཤེས་ནས་མིང་བཞིའི་ཕུང་པོས་བསྡུས་པའི་སྲིད་པའི་བར་དུ་འབྱུང་ལ། གང་དང་གང་དུ་སྐྱེས་ཀྱང་དེའི་སྐྱེ་བ་དང་རྒ་ཤི་འབྱུང་སྟེ། སླར་ཡང་ལས་ཉོན་གྱིས་འཕངས་ནས་སྐྱེ་བ་གཞན་ལེན་པས། དེ་ལྟར་མགལ་མེའི་འཁོར་ལོ་དང་ཟོ་ཆུན་ཁྱུད་མོ་ལྟར་ཁམས་གསུམ་སྲིད་པར་ཡང་ནས་ཡང་དུ་འཁོར་ཞིང་འཁྱམ་པར་འགྱུར་རོ།

།དེ་ལྟར་རྒྱུན་ཆགས་སུ་འབྱུང་ཚུལ་སྤྱིར་ཤེས་པར་བྱས་ནས་ཚེ་དུ་ལ་རྫོགས་དཔྱད་ན་སྔོན་དང་། ད་ལྟ་ཕྱི་མའི་སྐྱེ་བ་གསུམ་ལ་རྫོགས་ཚུལ་བཤད་མ་ཐག་པ་ལྟར་དང་། ཚེ་སྔོན་མའི་གནས་སྐབས་ཀྱི་ཕུང་པོས་བསྡུས་པའི་མ་རིག་པ་དང་། སྲིད་ལེན་གྱི་དབང་གིས་ལས་འདུ་བྱེད་པ་དག་གིས་འཕངས་པའི་ཕྱི་མའི་སྐྱེ་བ་ལེན་ཞིང་དེ་ལ་རྣམ་ཤེས་ནས་སྲིད་པའི་བར་དང་རྒ་ཤི་ཡང་འབྱུང་བས་ཚེ་གཉིས་ཀྱིས་རྫོགས་པའང་ཡོད་དོ།

[4,28] Thus, the one who possesses the acceptance that these [beliefs] will not arise in the future, will be confirmed in unexcelled enlightenment by all the buddhas.

[4,29] In this way, these twelve aspects of interdependence will continuously evolve for as long as ignorance has not been relinquished. The past causes, ignorance and formation, make the present consciousness that is the impelled result appear, and the following links, down to the disturbing emotions craving and grasping, gather the karma that produces a rebirth. Thus, up to becoming, eight evolve. Continuing therefrom, there is the taking of birth in the realm corresponding to one's karma and through that [bodily] support one will undergo the samsaric suffering of aging, dying and so forth.

[4,30] Concerning this support, for all the beings with form [the links] from consciousness until becoming will occur. If one is born in the Formless Realms, consciousness until becoming consisting of the four name aggregates will occur.

[4,31] Whenever or as whatever one has taken rebirth, there will occur the processes of being born, aging and dying. And again, having been forced by karmas and disturbing emotions to take another birth, one circles and wanders again and again through the existences of the three realms, like a swirling fire brand or the rim of a water wheel.

[4,32] After having understood in general this way of a continual occurrence, if one examines how many lives it takes to complete [one cycle of twelve links], it is taught how they are completed within the three lifetimes of the previous, the present, and the following [life-time].

[4,33] Due to the power of the ignorance, craving and grasping comprised of the aggregates in one's former lifetime, one takes the following birth propelled by the formations of karma. Since in that [life] consciousness until the [links of] becoming, old age and

།གང་ལྟར་ཡང་གཅིག་ལ་གཅིག་བརྟེན་ནས་རྒྱུན་ཆགས་པར་འབྱུང་བས་འདི་ལ་རྒྱུན་ཆགས་པའི་རྟེན་འབྲེལ་ཞེས་བྱའོ།

།གཞན་ཡང་བྱ་བ་རྫོགས་པའི་སྐད་ཅིག་ལ་བཅུ་གཉིས་ཚང་ཚུལ། སྲོག་གཅོད་པ་ལྟ་བུ་ལ་མཚོན་ན། མི་ཤེས་པས་འཇུག་པ་མ་རིག་པ། དེ་བཞིན་དུ་ལས་དེ་འདུ་བྱེད་པ། དེ་དུས་ཀྱི་ཤེས་པ་འབྱུང་བ། དེ་དུས་ཀྱི་མིང་གཟུགས་དང་། སྐྱེ་མཆེད་དྲུག་མཚོན་བསྟུན་པ་སོགས་ཀྱི་རིག་པ། དེ་དུས་རང་གཞན་གྱི་བདེ་སྡུག་མྱོང་ཞིང་ཚོར་བ། དེ་ལ་དགའ་བས་འཇུག་ཅིང་སྲེད་པ། དེ་ལས་ཕྱི་མའི་ཆ་དང་དུ་ལེན་པ། ལས་བྱེད་དུས་ཀྱི་ཕུང་པོ་སྲིད་པ། དེ་ལས་ད་ལྟ་དང་ཕྱི་མའི་ཆ་སྐྱེ་བ། དེ་འགྱུར་ཞིང་འགག་པ་རྒ་ཤིའི་ཡན་ལག་གི་ཚུལ་དུ་འདོད་དེ་སྐད་ཅིག་མའི་རྟེན་འབྲེལ་ལོ།

།རྒྱུན་ཆགས་པའི་རྟེན་འབྲེལ་ཡན་ལག་བཅུ་གཉིས་པོ་དེ་དག་བསྡུ་ན། མ་རིག་པ་དང་འདུ་བྱེད་དང་རྣམ་ཤེས་གསུམ་ནི་འཕེན་པའི་ཡན་ལག། མིང་གཟུགས་ནས་ཚོར་བའི་བར་བཞི་འཕངས་འབྲས་ཀྱི་ཡན་ལག། སྲེད་ལེན་སྲིད་པ་གསུམ་མངོན་པར་འགྲུབ་པའི་ཡན་ལག། སྐྱེ་བ་དང་རྒ་ཤི་གཉིས་མངོན་པར་གྲུབ་བའི་ཡན་ལག་སྟེ་བཞིར་འགྱུར་རོ།

།ཡང་གསུམ་དུ་སྡུད་དེ་མ་རིག་པ་དང་སྲེད་པ་དང་ལེན་པ་གསུམ་ནི་ཉོན་མོངས་པའོ། འདུ་བྱེད་དང་སྲིད་པ་གཉིས་ནི་ལས་སོ། །ལྷག་མ་བདུན་ནི་སྡུག་བསྔལ་གྱི་གཞི་བདུན་ནོ།

death evolve, [the twelve links] are also completed within two lifetimes.

[4,34] Whichever is the case, since there is a continual occurrence, one dependent upon the other, the process is called continuous interdependence.

[4,35] Moreover, there is also the manner in which the twelve [links] are contained within the moment of completing an act. When illustrating this with, for instance, the act of killing, to engage therein through lack of understanding is ignorance. Likewise, the action [karma] is formation. The cognition at that time is consciousness. The contact of the weapon piercing [the body] is the name-and-form and of the six sources present at that time. The experience or sensation at the time is the pleasure of oneself and pain of the other. There is enthusiastic engagement and craving, and from that comes the grasping of the following part. The aggregates at the time of committing the act is becoming, resulting in the birth of the present and following part. Their change and cessation are regarded as being the links of old age and death. Thus this is the continuous interdependence of a moment [of completing an act].

[4,36] When the twelve links of interdependence are condensed, the three [links] consisting of ignorance, formation and consciousness are the propelling links. The four from name-and-form to sensation are the links of the propelled result. The three [links] of craving, grasping and becoming are the fully establishing links, and the two of birth and old age and death are the fully established links. Thus there are four [subdivisions].

[4,37] They can also be divided into three: The three of ignorance, craving and grasping are disturbing emotions. The two of formation and becoming are karma. The remaining seven are the seven bases of suffering. These three categories are respectively called affliction of disturbing emotion, affliction of karma, and

འདི་གསུམ་ལ་རིམ་བ་ལྟར་ཉོན་མོངས་པས་ཀུན་ནས་ཉོན་མོངས་ལས་ཀྱི་ཀུན་ནས་ཉོན་མོངས་པ། ཚེའམ་སྐྱེ་བའི་ཀུན་ནས་ཉོན་མོངས་པ་ཞེས་འདོགས་ཏེ་འགྲོ་བ་རྣམས་ཉོན་མོངས་པར་བྱེད་པའི་ཕྱིར་རོ།

།ཡང་རིམ་པ་ལྟར་ཉོན་མོངས་པའི་གཞན་དབང་དང་། ལས་ཀྱི་གཞན་དབང་དང་། སྡུག་བསྔལ་གྱི་གཞན་དབང་ཞེས་ཀྱང་བརྗོད་དོ།

།ཉོན་མོངས་གསུམ་ལས་ལས་གཉིས་འབྱུང་ལ། དེ་ལས་སྡུག་བསྔལ་གྱི་གཞི་བདུན་འབྱུང་ཞིང་། བདུན་པོ་ལས་སླར་ཡང་ཉོན་མོངས་དང་ལས་འབྱུང་སྟེ་དེ་ལྟར་རྒྱུན་གྱིས་འཁོར་རོ།

།ཡན་ལག་བཅུ་གཉིས་ཀྱི་ནང་ནས་ལས་ཉོན་ལྔ་དང་རྣམ་ཤེས་རྣམས་ནི་ཡན་ལག་གཞན་རྣམས་སྒྲུབ་པར་བྱེད་པའི་རྒྱུ་སྟེ། མ་རིག་པ་དང་། ལས་དང་། སྲེད་པ་དང་། རྣམ་ཤེས་བཞིའོ། སྲེད་ལེན་གཉིས་སྲེད་པ་དང་། འདུ་བྱེད་སྲིད་པ་གཉིས་ལས་ཡིན་ནོ།

།དེ་ལ་རྣམ་ཤེས་ནི་ས་བོན་ལྟ་བུ། ལས་ཞིང་ས། སྲེད་པ་རླན། མ་རིག་པ་འདེབས་བྱེད་དང་ལུད་ལྟ་བུ་སྟེ། དེ་བཞིས་སྲིད་པའི་སྐྱེ་གནས་རྣམས་སུ་མིང་གཟུགས་ཀྱི་མྱུ་གུ་འགྲུབ་པར་བྱེད་དོ།

།ལུགས་འབྱུང་གི་རྟེན་འབྲེལ་དེ་དག་བསྡུས་ན་ལས་ཉོན་ལྔ་ནི་རྒྱུ་ཀུན་འབྱུང་གི་བདེན་པས་བསྡུས་ལ། ལྷག་མ་བདུན་ནི་སྡུག་བདེན་གྱིས་བསྡུས་པའོ།

།ལུགས་ལྡོག་གི་དབང་དུ་བྱས་ན་བདེན་པའི་ཆོས་ཉིད་རྟོགས་པའི་ཡེ་ཤེས་ཀྱིས་མ་རིག་པ་སྤངས་ནས་ལས་ཉོན་ལྔ་ལྡོག་པ་ལམ་བདེན་དང་། སྡུག་བསྔལ་གྱི་གཞི་བདུན་དེ་བཞིན་ཉིད་དུ་འགོག་པ་འགོག་བདེན་ཏེ་བདེན་དོན་རྣམ་པ་བཅུ་གཉིས་ཀྱི་རང་བཞིན་ནོ།

།དེ་ལྟར་རྟེན་ཅིང་འབྲེལ་བར་འབྱུང་བ་འདི་ནི་སངས་རྒྱས་ཀྱི་གསུང་གི་མཛོད་ཀྱི་ནང་ན་གཅེས་

affliction of life or rebirth, because they afflict all sentient beings. Again, they are also respectively called dependency of disturbing emotion, dependency of karma, and dependency of suffering.

[4,38] From the three disturbing emotions come the two karmas, and from these arise the seven bases of suffering. From these seven again arise the disturbing emotions and karmas. Thus one continuously circles around [within samsara].

[4,39] Among the twelve links, the five disturbing emotions and karmas and the consciousness are the causes which form all the other links. Thus there can be said to be four links: ignorance, karma, craving, and consciousness. Here both craving and grasping are [defined as] craving, and both formation and becoming as karma.

[4,40] To explain this further, understand consciousness to be like a seed, karma like a field, craving like moisture, and ignorance like planting and manure. These four produce the sprouts of name-and-form in all the birthplaces of becoming.

[4,41] When these interdependent links, in progressive order, are condensed, the five karmas and disturbing emotions are included under the truth of origin and the remaining seven fall under the truth of suffering.

[4,42] In terms of reverse order, having relinquished ignorance through the wisdom that realizes the nature of the truths, the reversal of the five that are karmas and disturbing emotions is the truth of path. Likewise, the ceasing of the seven bases of suffering is the truth of cessation. Thus they are the nature of the twelvefold points of truth.

[4,43] In that way, dependent origination ranks as an essential and profound teaching among the treasuries of the Buddha's Words. The one who perceives dependent origination with the eyes of discriminating knowledge will come to see the dharmas possessing the natures of the eightfold noble path, and with the wisdom

པ་ཟབ་མོར་གྱུར་པ་སྟེ། སུས་ཤེས་རབ་ཀྱི་སྤྱན་གྱིས་རྟེན་ཅིང་འབྲེལ་བར་འབྱུང་བ་མཐོང་བ་དེས་འཕགས་ལམ་བརྒྱད་ཀྱི་རང་བཞིན་ཅན་གྱི་ཆོས་མཐོང་ཞིང་། ཡེ་ཤེས་ཀྱི་གཟིགས་པས་ཤེས་བྱ་ཐམས་ཅད་ཐུགས་སུ་ཆུད་པ་སངས་རྒྱས་ཆོས་ཀྱི་སྐུ་མཐོང་བ་ཡིན་ནོ། །ཞེས་གསུངས་སོ།

།རྟེན་འབྲེལ་གྱི་སྐབས་སོ།

gaze which comprehends all objects of knowledge will perceive the dharmakaya of buddhahood. Thus it has been taught.

[4,44] This was the chapter on interdependence.

།གནས་དང་གནས་མ་ཡིན་པ་ནི་ཤེས་བྱ་ཐམས་ཅད་ལ་ཁྱབ་པ་སྟེ།

རྒྱུ་གང་ལས་གང་འབྱུང་མི་འབྱུང་གི་ཁྱད་པར། དགེ་བའི་ལས་ལས་བདེ་བ་འབྱུང་ཞིང་སྡུག་བསྔལ་མི་འབྱུང་བ་དང་། འབྲས་ཀྱི་ས་བོན་ལས་རང་གི་མྱུ་གུ་སྐྱེ་ལ་ནས་ཀྱི་མྱུ་གུ་མི་སྐྱེ་བ་ལྟ་བུ་དང་། གང་བདག་མེད་པར་རྟོགས་པ་ལས་ཐར་པ་ཐོབ་བ་གནས་ཡིན་ལ། བདག་ཡོད་པར་འཛིན་པ་ལས་ཐར་བ་ཐོབ་པ་གནས་མིན་པ་ལྟ་བུ་དང་།

མི་ཚ་བ་ཡིན་ཞིང་དེ་ལ་གྲང་བ་གནས་མེད་པ་ལྟ་བུ་ཤེས་བྱ་ཐམས་ཅད་ཀྱི་རང་བཞིན་ལ་གནས་དང་གནས་མིན་སྣ་ཚོགས་ཡོད་དོ།

།དེ་མཚོན་བྱེད་ཙམ་དུ་གཞན་དབང་བདུན་གསུངས་ཏེ།

མི་འདོད་པ་གཞན་དབང་མི་དགེའི་ལས་ཀྱིས་ངན་འགྲོར་འགྲོ་བ་ལྟ་བུ།

འདོད་པ་གཞན་དབང་དགེ་བའི་ལས་ཀྱིས་བདེ་འགྲོར་སྐྱེ་བ་ལྟ་བུ།

རྣམ་པར་དག་པ་གཞན་དབང་སྒྲིབ་པ་མ་སྤངས་པར་རྣམ་དག་མི་འཐོབ་པ་ལྟ་བུ།

མཉམ་དུ་འབྱུང་བ་གཞན་དབང་འགྲན་ཟླ་མེད་པའི་ལས་བསགས་པས་སངས་རྒྱས་དང་འཁོར་སྒྱུར་རེ་རེ་ལས་ཟུང་རེ་ལྷན་ཅིག་མི་འབྱུང་བ་ལྟ་བུ།

དབང་བྱེད་པ་གཞན་དབང་བུད་མེད་ཀྱི་རྟེན་གྱིས་འཁོར་ལོ་སོགས་རིན་ཆེན་སྣ་བདུན་ལ་དབང་བྱེད་མི་ནུས་པ་ལྟ་བུ།

5
The Correct and the Incorrect

[5,1] The categories of what is correct and incorrect encompass all objects of knowledge. They are the difference between what results and what does not result from a certain cause. For instance, it is correct that pleasure results from a virtuous action and not pain; and that from a grain of rice grows a rice sprout, rather than a barley sprout. It is correct that the person who realizes the absence of a self attains liberation, while it is incorrect that someone who holds the existence of a self attains liberation.

[5,2] It is correct that fire is hot, and incorrect that it is cold. As in these examples, all objects of knowledge by nature encompass various categories of what is correct and incorrect.

[5,3] To roughly outline this, seven dependencies are taught:

1) Dependency of the undesired is, for example, to go to the lower realms due to unvirtuous actions.[13]

2) Dependency of the desired is, for example, to be reborn in the happy states through virtuous actions.

3) Dependency of purity is, for example, that one will not attain total purity without relinquishing the obscurations.

4) Dependency of co-occurrence is, for example, that by having accumulated matchless karma, a buddha and a world ruler only appear individually and not together at the same time.

5) Dependency of control is, for example, that through the physical body of a woman, one is unable to take possession of the

འཐོབ་པ་གཞན་དབང་བུད་མེད་ཀྱི་རྟེན་ལ་རང་སངས་རྒྱས་མི་ཐོབ་པ་ལྟ་བུ། ཀུན་ཏུ་སྤྱོད་པ་གཞན་དབང་འཕགས་པས་སྲོག་གཅོད་སོགས་མི་སྤྱོད་པ་ལྟ་བུ་སྟེ།

།འདི་དག་ནི་གནས་དང་གནས་མིན་གྱི་གཞན་དབང་གིས་བྱས་ཀྱིས། རང་གང་འདོད་དུ་ཅི་དགར་བྱེད་དུ་མེད་པ་ནི་དངོས་པོའི་ཆོས་ཉིད་ཡིན་ནོ་ཞེས་བསྟན་པ་འདིས་མཚོན་ནས། ཆོས་རྣམས་ལ་གང་དང་ཅི་ཞིག་གནས་ཡོད་པ་དང་། མེད་པ་ཤེས་པར་བྱ་སྟེ། རྒྱུ་ཀུན་འབྱུང་ལས་སྡུག་བསྔལ་འབྱུང་བ་དང་། ལམ་ལས་འགོག་པ་འབྱུང་བ་སོགས་གནས་ཡོད་དང་། ལམ་ལས་སྡུག་བསྔལ་དང་། ཀུན་འབྱུང་ལས་འགོག་པ་འབྱུང་བ་གནས་མེད་སོགས་རྟེན་ཅིང་འབྲེལ་འབྱུང་གི་ཚུལ་གྱིས་བདེན་བཞིའི་འཇུག་ལྡོག་གིས་བསྡུས་པ་ཐམས་ཅད་ཀྱང་འདིའི་ཁོངས་སུ་འདུ་སྟེ།

།མདོར་ན་ཤེས་བྱ་རིག་པའི་གནས་ཐམས་ཅད་གནས་དང་གནས་མིན་ཤེས་པའི་ཆེད་དུ་ཡིན་ཏེ། བཟོ་རིག་པས་གང་ལ་བྱ་བའི་དོན་ལེགས་པ་དང་མི་ལེགས་པའི་གནས་སྐབས་ཤེས་པར་བྱེད་པ་དང་།

གསོ་དཔྱད་ཀྱི་རིག་པས་ནད་ཞི་བ་དང་མི་ཞི་བའི་གཉེན་པོ་སོགས་ཤེས་པ་དང་།

སྒྲ་རིག་པས་མིང་སོགས་ཀྱི་རང་བཞིན་དང་། དེ་ལ་སྦྱོར་བའི་རྐྱེན་དང་། དེ་ལས་རྣམ་འགྱུར་ཇི་ལྟར་བྱ་བའི་གནས་གནས་མིན་ཤེས་པར་བྱེད་པ་དང་།

ཚད་མ་རིག་པས་བསྒྲུབ་བྱ་གང་ཞིག་སྒྲུབ་བྱེད་གང་ལས་འགྲུབ་མི་འགྲུབ་གྱི་ཚུལ་ཤེས་པ་དང་།

precious wheel and the other of the seven precious possessions [of a universal monarch].

6) Dependency of attainment is, for example, that one does not attain the state of a pratyekabuddha in the physical body of a woman.

7) Dependency of behavior is, for example, that a noble being does not engage in [negative] acts such as killing.

[5,4] It is the nature of things that these take place through the dependency of what is correct and incorrect, rather than as one desires or feels like. Understand hereby that all phenomena, whatever they may be, possess aspects of what is correct and what is not.

[5,5] It is correct that suffering results from the cause of the [truth of] origin, and that cessation results from the path. It is incorrect that suffering results from the path and that cessation results from origin [of suffering]. Thus, everything comprised of the progression and reversal of the four truths through dependent origination is included herein.

[5,6] In short, all the sciences of knowledge are meant for understanding what is correct and what is incorrect.

[5,7] By the science of craftsmanship one understands the situation in which a created object is excellent or not excellent.

[5,8] By the science of healing and diagnosis one comes to know the remedy which cures or does not cure an illness.

[5,9] By the science of language one understands what is correct and incorrect for the character of words, the conditions for combining them, and how they form their inflections.

[5,10] By the science of logic one comes to know the manner in which a certain predicate is established or not established from a certain proof.[14]

ནང་རིག་པས་དངོས་པོའི་དེ་ཉིད་ཤེས་ཤིང་དོན་དུ་གཉེར་བྱའི་གཙོ་བོ་ལམ་དང་འགོག་པ་ཡང་དག་པར་ཤེས་པར་བྱེད་པ་དང་། དེ་བཞིན་དུ་མངོན་བརྗོད་ཀྱིས་དོན་གང་ལ་མིང་སྣ་ཚོགས་འཇུག་མི་འཇུག རྩིས་ཀྱིས་གྲངས་སོགས་ཇི་ལྟ་བུས་གནས། ཟློས་གར་གྱིས་སྐད་རིགས་སྣ་ཚོགས། སྙན་ངག་གིས་བརྗོད་པ་མཛེས་མི་མཛེས། སྡེབ་སྦྱོར་གྱིས་ཚིགས་བཅད་ཀྱི་ལྡུ་ཡང་སོགས་ཀྱི་གནས་གནས་མིན་ཤེས་པར་བྱེད་པ་ཡིན་མོད་ཀྱི། འདིར་ནི་ནང་རིག་པ་ལས་གྲུབ་པའི་མཐའ་མདོར་བསྡུས་པ་ཙམ་ཞིག་བཤད་པར་བྱ་སྟེ། དེ་ཤེས་ན་གནས་གནས་མིན་གྱི་དོན་ལ་མཁས་པར་འགྱུར་བའི་ཕྱིར་རོ།

།དེ་ཡང་གྲུབ་པའི་མཐའ་ལ་སྤང་བྱ་ཕྱི་རོལ་པ་དང་། བླང་བྱ་ནང་པ་གཉིས། ཕྱི་ནང་ཙམ་གྱི་ཁྱད་པར་དཀོན་མཆོག་གསུམ་སྐྱབས་གནས་ཡང་དག་ཏུ་ཁས་ལེན་མི་ལེན་གྱིས་འབྱེད་དོ།

།དེ་དག་གི་གྲུབ་མཐའ་ལ། ཕྱི་རོལ་པ་ལ་ལྟ་བ་དྲུག་ཅུ་རྩ་གཉིས་སོགས་དབྱེ་སྒོ་མང་ཡང་།
བསྡུ་ན་ཏཀྐ་སྡེ་ལྔར་འདུ་ཞིང་སོ་སོའི་འདོད་ཚུལ་མང་དུ་ཡོད་ལ།
དེ་ཐམས་ཅད་ཀྱི་རྩ་བ་བསྡུས་ན་རྟག་ཆད་སྨྲ་བ་གཉིས་སུ་འདུའོ།

།དེ་ལ་རྟག་སྨྲ་བ་རྣམས་ཀྱིས་བདག་དང་དུས་དང་དབང་ཕྱུག་ཚངས་པ་ཁྱབ་འཇུག་སོགས་གང་ཡིན་པ་དེ་འཇིག་རྟེན་ཀུན་གྱི་བྱེད་པ་པོར་ལྟ་ཞིང་དེ་ཉིད་རྟག་པར་འདོད། རྟག་པ་དེ་འདྲ་བའི་གོ་འཕང་ཐོབ་ཕྱིར་ལྷ་མཆོད་པར་བྱེད་པ་དང་བསམ་གཏན་སྒོམ་པ་སོགས་ཀྱི་ལམ་ཡོད་དོ།

[5,11] By the inner science one understands the nature of things[15] and comes to perfectly know the main object of pursuit, the path and cessation.

[5,12] Likewise, by the science of synonyms, one understands how various words will or will not apply to a certain meaning; by the science of mathematics, the correctness of how various numbers and so on are; by the science of performance, the different tones of voice; by the science of poetry, whether an expression is beautiful or not; and by the science of composition one will come to understand what is correct or is incorrect concerning the sketchiness or verbosity of a sentence.

[5,13] Here I shall only briefly explain the philosophical schools according to the inner science. Understanding of them will cause one to be learned in the meaning of what is correct or incorrect.

[5,14] There are two kinds of philosophical schools: those of the outsiders, which are to be abandoned, and those of the insiders [Buddhists], which are to be adopted. The difference between outsiders and insiders lies in whether or not the Three Jewels are accepted as being perfect objects of refuge.[16]

[5,15] Among these philosophical schools, there are numerous divisions of outsiders such as the sixty-two views. There are many ways of classifying them, but they can be condensed into the Five Tarka Groups.[17]

[5,16] Although these again have many different beliefs, when condensing the root of all of them, there are two: proponents of eternalism and proponents of nihilism.

[5,17] The proponents of eternalism believe that either the Self, Time, the Almighty, Brahma, or Vishnu is the creator of the entire world. They hold that this creator is permanent.[18] In order to achieve this state of permanence they have the paths of pleasing the godhead, practicing meditation and so forth.

།ཆད་པར་སྨྲ་བ་རྣམས་ཀྱིས་སྔོན་གྱི་ལས་སོགས་ཀྱི་རྒྱུ་མེད་པར་ད་ལྟའི་འཇིག་རྟེན་འདི་རང་གི་ངོ་བོས་བྱུང་སྟེ། སེམས་ནི་འབྱུང་བ་བཞི་ལས་གློ་བུར་དུ་བྱུང་ཞིང་། འཆི་བའི་དུས་ན་རྒྱུན་ཆད་པས་ཐར་པ་སྒྲུབ་ཕྱིར་ལམ་ལ་འབད་པ་སོགས་དོན་མེད་དོ་ཞེས་ཟེར།

།འདི་ཀུན་ཀྱང་བདག་ཡོད་པར་སྨྲ་བ་ཡིན་ནོ།

།དེ་ལ་སངས་རྒྱས་པས་དཔྱད་ན། རྒྱུ་རྟག་པ་དེ་འདྲས་འཇིག་རྟེན་སྐྱེད་པའི་དོན་མི་བྱེད་དེ། འཇིག་རྟེན་ཐམས་ཅད་ཅིག་ཆར་བསྐྱེད་པར་མ་དམིགས་ལ། རིམ་གྱིས་བསྐྱེད་ན་རྒྱུ་མི་རྟག་པར་འགྱུར་རོ།

།ཡང་བྱེད་པ་པོ་དེ་ལ་རྒྱུ་གཞན་ཡོད་ན་བྱེད་པོ་ཐུག་མེད་དུ་འགྱུར་ཞིང་མི་རྟག་པར་ཡང་འགྱུར་བ་དང་། མེད་ན་དེ་ཡོད་པའི་རྒྱུ་མཚན་བསྒྲུབ་དུ་མེད་པར་འགྱུར་བ་དང་། ཡང་དེས་བསམ་བཞིན་བྱེད་ན་བསམ་བའི་གཞན་དབང་ཅན་དང་མི་རྟག་པར་འགྱུར་ལ། སེམས་ཅན་སྡུག་བསྔལ་ཅན་བྱེད་པ་མི་རིགས་པ་བྱེད་པར་འགྱུར་རོ།

།བསམ་བཞིན་མི་བྱེད་ན་རང་དབང་མེད་པ་དང་། དེ་མཆོད་ཀྱང་ཕན་པར་མི་འགྱུར་བ་སོགས་རིགས་པ་ཡང་དག་གི་སྒོ་དུ་མས་ཁེགས་པ་ཡིན་ནོ།

རྒྱུ་མེད་པར་འབྱུང་བ་མི་སྲིད་དེ། གལ་ཏེ་འབྱུང་ན་དེ་འདྲ་ཡུལ་དུས་ཀུན་ན་རྟག་ཏུ་ཁྱད་མེད་པར་ཡོད་པར་འགྱུར་ཏེ། རྒྱུ་མེད་ཀྱང་ཆོས་རྣམས་ཀྱི་རང་གི་ངོ་བོ་སྲིད་པར་འདོད་པའི་ཕྱིར་རོ།

།ཡང་ན་སྐྱུ་རུ་སོགས་ཡུལ་དང་དུས་གང་ན་ཡང་མེད་པར་འགྱུར་ཏེ། ས་བོན་དང་ཆུ་སོགས་ཚོགས་ཀྱང་དེའི་རྒྱུ་མ་ཡིན་པར་འདོད་པའི་ཕྱིར་དེ་གང་གིས་ཀྱང་སྐྱེད་པ་མེད་པའི་ཕྱིར་རོ།

[5,18] The proponents of nihilism claim that the present world originated by itself without causes, such as past karma; that consciousness occurred suddenly from the four elements; and that since it is discontinued at the time of death, it is pointless to exert oneself on the path in order to achieve liberation. All of these [nihilists] are, however, proponents of the existence of a self.[19]

[5,19] When these beliefs are scrutinized by a Buddhist, [it is seen that] such a permanent cause cannot perform the function of creating the world. This is because you cannot find that the whole world was created simultaneously, but only gradually. Consequently its cause is not permanent.[20]

Or, if its creator were itself to have another cause, there would be no end to creators, and again the creator would not be permanent. If the creator were to be causeless, on the other hand, it would be impossible to establish a reason for its existence.

Moreover, if it [the godhead, etc.] creates intentionally, it is dependent upon intention and consequently is not permanent. It is also unreasonable that it would create suffering sentient beings. If the creator were not to create intentionally, it would lack independent control, and consequently there would be no benefit even if one were to worship it. In these and other ways, the concept of a creator is refuted by means of correct reasoning.

[5,20] Origination without a cause is impossible. If it were possible, something should be able to originate in the same way in all places and at all times without any difference. The reason should follow the claim that all phenomena, even without having causes, exist by virtue of their own nature.[21]

Or, a sprout, for instance, will not be able to exist at a certain time and place. This should follow the claim that a seed and water and so forth are not causes [of the sprout], since they do not [necessarily] produce anything even if they come together.

།དེ་ལྟ་ན་ཡང་དངོས་པོ་རྣམས་ནི་གང་དུ་རྒྱུ་རྐྱེན་ཚོགས་པའི་ཡུལ་དུས་དེ་ན་ཡོད་ཅིང༌། མ་ཚོགས་པ་ན་མེད་པས་རེས་འགའ་བ་ཡིན་པའི་ཕྱིར་རྒྱུ་ལས་བྱུང་བར་གྲུབ་བོ།

།ཡང་འབྱུང་བ་བཞི་ལས་རྣམ་ཤེས་གསར་དུ་འབྱུང་ངོ་ཞེས་འདོད་ན། རང་གིས་ཆོས་རྣམས་རྒྱུ་མེད་དུ་ཁས་བླངས་པ་ཡང་ཉམས་ལ།

ད་ལྟའི་རྣམ་ཤེས་ནི་རང་གི་ཉེར་ལེན་གྱི་རྒྱུ་རྣམ་ཤེས་སྔ་མ་ལས་སྐྱེ་ཞིང་རྒྱུན་འཇུག་པར་མཐོང་བའི་ཕྱིར། སྔར་རང་གི་ཉེར་ལེན་གྱི་རྒྱུ་མེད་པར་བེམ་པོ་ལས་འབྱུང་མི་སྲིད་དེ། རྡོ་ལས་མྱུ་གུ་དང༌། སྨུན་པ་ལས་སྣང་བ་བཞིན་ནོ།

།རྣམ་ཤེས་གསལ་རིག་གི་རྒྱུན་འདི་ཀློག་སོགས་བྱུང་བ་ལྟར་སྔ་མ་སྔ་མ་ལས་ཕྱི་མ་ཕྱི་མ་དག་འབྱུང་ཞིང་རྒྱུན་མི་འཆད་པར་མཐོང་ན་རྒྱུ་ཚང་བཞིན་འཆི་བའི་ཚེ་ཇི་ལྟར་རྒྱུན་ཆད་པར་འགྱུར་ཏེ། ས་བོན་སྐྱོན་མེད་པ་ས་ཆུ་སོགས་ཀྱི་རྐྱེན་དང་ལྡན་པའམ། ཀླུང་ཆེན་པོའི་རྒྱུན་འཇུག་པ་བཞིན་ནོ།

།དེ་ལྟར་བརྟག་ན་ཆོས་ཐམས་ཅད་ནི་རང་རང་གི་རྒྱུ་ཡོད་ན་སྐྱེ་ལ་མེད་ན་མི་སྐྱེ་བས་རྟེན་ཅིང་འབྲེལ་བར་འབྱུང་བ་ཉིད་དུ་དངོས་སྟོབས་ཀྱི་རིགས་པས་མཐོང་བའི་ཕྱིར། དབང་ཕྱུག་སོགས་ཀྱི་རྒྱུ་ལས་མ་ཡིན་ཞིང༌། རྒྱུ་མེད་པར་ཡང་མིན་ནོ།

།དེ་ལྟ་བས་ན་རྟེན་ནས་འབྱུང་བའི་ཕུང་པོ་ལྔ་པོ་འདི་ལ་བདག་དང་བྱེད་པ་པོ་མེད་དེ་ཕུང་པོ་དང་གཅིག་ཐ་དད་གང་དུ་ཡང་མ་དམིགས་པས་སོ།

[5,21] This being so, all things exist in a certain place and time where and when their causes and condition have come together. They do not exist without these [causes and conditions] coming together. Since this [presence and absence] alternates, it is established that [all things] originate from causes.

[5,22] Maintaining that consciousness originates as something new from the four elements counteracts the [nihilistic] claim that all phenomena are without causes.

Since the present consciousness is seen to occur and continue from the previous [instant of] consciousness, its own perpetuating cause, it is impossible that it should originate from [dead] matter, without its own former perpetuating cause. This would be as [impossible as] a sprout [growing] from stone or light [appearing] from darkness.

[5,23] It is seen that the aware and cognizant continuity of consciousness originates and occurs without interruption, the next moment resulting from the previous, just as one progresses steadily when training in reading and other things. How, then, can it be discontinued at the time of death, while its own [perpetuating] causes are still present? This is like [the example of] a flawless seed possessing the conditions such as earth and water, or like the continuous flow of a great river.[22]

[5,24] When examining in this way one sees, through factual reasoning, that phenomena originate in dependent connection when their individual causes are present, and do not arise when their causes are absent. Consequently, they do not arise from a cause such as the Almighty; neither do they arise without a cause.

[5,25] For these reasons, the five aggregates which are dependent-arising are devoid of a self and a creator, because neither of these attributes are found to be identical with or different from the aggregates.

།ནང་པའི་གྲུབ་མཐའ་བྱེ་མདོ་དབུ་སེམས་བཞི་ལས།

བྱེ་བྲག་སྨྲ་བས་ཤེས་བྱ་གཞི་ལྔ་དང་དུས་གསུམ་སོགས་རྫས་ཡོད་དུ་འདོད་དེ། གཞི་གྲུབ་པ་རྣམས་དེ་དང་དེའི་ཆོས་སུ་ཡོད་པས་ཐམས་ཅད་ཡོད་པར་འདོད།

དེ་ལ་བཙོམ་པའམ་བློས་གཞན་བསལ་ན་གཞིག་ཏུ་རུང་བ་བུམ་པ་ལྟ་བུ་ལ་སོགས་པ་ཀུན་རྫོབ་ཏུ་ཡོད་པ་དང་། གཞིག་ཏུ་མེད་པ་རྡུལ་ཕྲ་རབ་དང་སྐད་ཅིག་ཆ་མེད་གཉིས་ནི་དོན་དམ་དུ་ཡོད་པ་སྟེ་དངོས་པོ་ཀུན་གྱི་རྩོམ་གཞིའོ།

།ཀུན་རྫོབ་དོན་དམ་དུ་ཡོད་པ་གཉིས་ཀ་ཡང་ཆོས་རང་རང་གི་ངོ་བོ་རྫས་སུ་ཡོད་པས་མི་སྟོང་པར་འདོད།

གང་ཟག་གི་བདག་ནི་ཕུང་པོ་ལས་གཅིག་ཐ་དད་དུ་མེད་པས་རྫས་སུ་མེད་པ་དང་། མིག་དབང་སོགས་ལ་བརྟེན་པའི་ཤེས་པས་རང་དང་དུས་མཉམ་པའི་ཡུལ་རྣམ་མེད་རྗེན་ཅེར་དུ་འཛིན་པ་དང་། རང་རིག་མི་འདོད་པ་དང་། སྐྱེ་སོགས་མཚན་ཉིད་རྣམས་དངོས་པོ་ལས་ཐ་དད་པར་འདོད་པ་སོགས། ཐ་སྙད་འདོད་ཚུལ་དུ་མ་ཡོད་དོ།

།མདོ་སྡེ་པས་ནི་ཆ་མེད་གཉིས་དང་བདག་མེད་འདོད་ཚུལ་གོང་དང་འདྲ་ལ། ལྡན་མིན་འདུ་བྱེད་དང་འདུས་མ་བྱས་རྣམས་རྫས་སུ་གྲུབ་པ་མེད་དེ་ཀུན་བརྟགས་པ་ཙམ་མོ།

།ལྡན་མིན་ནི་བེམ་ཤེས་ཀྱི་གནས་སྐབས་ལ་བཏགས་པ་ཙམ་ལས་རང་གི་ངོ་བོ་རང་རྒྱ་ཐུབ་པར་ལོགས་སུ་མེད་ལ། འདུས་མ་བྱས་ནི་དགག་བྱ་བཅད་པ་ལས་བཏགས་པ་ཙམ་མོ།

[5,26] There are four Buddhist schools: Vaibhashika, Sautrantika, Mind Only, and Madhyamaka.

[5,27] The Vaibhashika proponents assert that the five bases of knowables and the three times have substantial existence. The established bases [of smallest atom and instant] are all held to exist because they possess their own attributes.

When a vase, for instance, is demolished or intellectually dissected, such a thing which can be broken into pieces has conventional existence. That which cannot be broken asunder, the two types of partless entities — the [partless] smallest particle and the partless instant [of consciousness] — have ultimate existence because they are the basic components for all things.

[5,28] Both conventional and ultimate existence are claimed not to be empty, because the identity of each phenomenon has a substantial existence.

The Vaibhashika proponents also maintain that the self of the individual has no substantial existence because it is neither identical with nor different from the aggregates. They accept that the consciousness supported by the eye faculty or the other [faculties] directly apprehends the object which is simultaneous with itself without a [mental] image [of that object]; that there is no self-knowing; and that all attributes such as arising [dwelling, and ceasing] are separate from the things themselves.

[5,29] In similar ways, they have numerous systems of accepted conventions.

[5,30] The way in which the Sautrantikas view the two types of partlessness and absence of the self [of the individual person] is the same as the above.

They, however, maintain that the nonconcurrent formations and the unconditioned things are merely imputations, having no substantial existence.

།སྔ་མའི་ཡུལ་དབང་ཤེས་གསུམ་ཚོགས་པའི་རྒྱུ་ལས་ད་ལྟ་བའི་མིག་ཤེས་སོགས་སྐྱེ་ཞིང་། ཤེས་པ་དེས་ཡུལ་གྱི་རྣམ་པ་བློ་ལ་ཤར་བ་དེ་འཛིན་གྱི་ཡུལ་དངོས་སུ་མི་འཛིན་ཏེ་ཡུལ་ནི་རྣམ་པ་གཏོད་བྱེད་ཀྱི་རྒྱུ་ཕྱོག་ན་ཡོད་པའོ།

།ཤེས་པ་ཐམས་ཅད་ཀྱིས་རང་རིག་པར་བྱེད་པ་དང་། དངོས་པོ་རྣམས་རྐྱེན་བཞི་ལས་སྐྱེ་ཞིང་རང་གི་ངོ་བོས་སྐད་ཅིག་གིས་འགག་པའི་ཆོས་ཅན་ཏེ། དངོས་པོ་དང་དེའི་མཚན་ཉིད་སྐྱེ་སོགས་ཐ་དད་དུ་མེད་དེ་ལྡོག་པའི་སྒོ་ནས་བཏགས་བ་ཙམ་དུ་འདོད་དོ།

།དེ་དག་ནི་ཕྱི་དོན་གཞལ་བ་ལ་དངོས་སྟོབས་ཀྱི་རིགས་པ་དང་ལྡན་ཞིང་། བཏགས་པ་རྣམས་ལ་རྫས་སུ་གྲུབ་པའི་ངོ་བོ་མེད་པར་རྟོགས་པ་སོགས་ཀྱིས་དངོས་པོའི་དོན་ལ་ཕྱིན་ཅི་མ་ལོག་པར་གཞལ་བའི་ཚུལ་འགར་ཞིག་གིས་བྱེད་སྨྲའི་གྲུབ་མཐའ་ལས་འཕགས་སོ།

།ལྡན་མིན་རྣམས་བཏགས་པ་ཡིན་ཀྱང་ཐ་སྙད་དོན་མཐུན་ཡིན་པས་དངོས་པོའི་སྟེང་ན་ཡོད་པའི་ཆོས་སུ་ཁས་ལེན་དགོས་ཏེ་བྱེ་སྨྲས་ཀུན་བརྟགས་འབའ་ཞིག་ཡིན་ན་དངོས་པོའི་སྟེང་ན་མི་རྟག་པ་མེད་པར་འགྱུར་བའི་གནོད་ཤེས་པར་བྱོས།

།དེ་བཞིན་དུ་ནམ་མཁའ་སོགས་འདུས་མ་བྱས་ཀྱང་ཐ་སྙད་དུ་ཡོད་པར་འདོད་དགོས་པ་ཡིན་ནོ།

[5,31] The nonconcurrent [formations] are mere imputations made when mind and matter [are together], and have no independent individual identity apart from that. The unconditioned things are only imputations resulting from an elimination of something negated.

[5,32] The present eye consciousness, for instance, occurs from the cause of the previous object, the faculty of sight and consciousness having come together. This consciousness then takes hold of the image of its object appearing in the mind, and not the actual object itself. Hence, the object, the cause that presents the image, has a hidden existence.

[5,33] They also accept that all the consciousnesses are self-knowing, and that all things arise from four conditions and have by nature the quality of ceasing instantly.

[5,34] Hence, a thing itself and its attributes such as arising [dwelling, and ceasing] are not separate, but merely imputations through opposition.

[5,35] The Sautrantikas have several ways of correctly evaluating the identity of things: by means of factual reasoning when evaluating outer objects, and by means of understanding that all imputations are devoid of an identity which has substantial existence. Hence, they are superior to the philosophical system of the Vaibhashikas.

[5,36] A vital point to understand is that although the nonconcurrent [formations] are imputed, since their names resemble their object, [the Sautrantikas] must accept that attributes exist in the things themselves. This is because, as the Vaibhashikas say, if the [attributes] were exclusively imputations, things would be devoid of [attributes such as] impermanence.

[5,37] In the same way, [the Sautrantikas] must also assert that the unconditioned things such as space have conventional existence.

[5,38] The [followers of the] Mind Only School hold that all these present appearances are just habitual tendencies of various kinds

།སེམས་ཙམ་པས་ནི། འདི་ལྟར་སྣང་བ་ཐམས་ཅད་ཐོག་མ་མེད་པའི་དུས་ནས་རྣམ་རྟོག་སྣ་ཚོགས་གོམས་པའི་བག་ཆགས་ཉིད་ཀུན་གཞིའི་རྣམ་ཤེས་ལ་བཞག་པ་དེ་ཉིད་ཀྱི་མཐུ་ལས་སེམས་ཀུན་གཞིའི་ཤེས་པ་ཉིད་གནས་དོན་ལུས་ཀྱི་སྣང་བའི་རྣམ་པ་ཉིད་དུ་ཤར་བ་མ་གཏོགས་གཞན་མེད་པས་ཐམས་ཅད་སེམས་ཀྱི་སྣང་བ་ཙམ་སྟེ། དཔེར་ན་རྨི་ལམ་གྱི་སྣང་བ་བཞིན་ནོ།

།ཞེས་པ་ལས་གཞན་པའི་ཕྱི་རོལ་གྱི་དོན་མ་གྲུབ་སྟེ། དངོས་པོ་རགས་པ་རྣམས་གསལ་བའི་མཐར་རྩོམ་གཞི་ཆ་མེད་གཉིས་ཀྱང་དོན་དམ་པར་མི་འགྲུབ་སྟེ། རྡུལ་ཆ་མེད་ཀྱིས་རགས་པ་རྩོམ་པའི་ཚེ། དབུས་རྡུལ་གཅིག་ལ་ཕྱོགས་རྡུལ་དྲུག་གམ་བཅུས་བསྐོར་བ་ན། རྡུལ་ཐ་དད་ཀྱིས་རེག་པའི་ཆ་རེ་ཡོད་ན་ཆ་བཅས་སུ་འགྱུར་ལ། མེད་ན་ཕྲ་རྡུལ་ཅི་ཙམ་ཚོགས་ཀྱང་ཇེ་ཆེར་རྒྱས་པར་མི་འགྱུར་བས་ཆ་མེད་གཞིག་ཏུ་མི་རུང་བ་མ་གྲུབ་སྟེ་བཏགས་པ་ཙམ་དུ་འགྱུར་རོ།

།དུས་མཐའི་ཆ་མེད་ཀྱང་། རང་གི་སྔ་ཕྱིའི་ཆ་མེད་ལ་ཕྱོགས་པའི་ཆ་ཐ་དད་ཡོད་ན་ཆ་བཅས་སུ་འགྱུར་ལ། མེད་ན་དུས་མཐའི་སྐད་ཅིག་དུ་ཙམ་བསགས་ཀྱང་རྒྱུན་རིང་བར་མི་འགྱུར་ཏེ་སྐད་ཅིག་ཙམ་དུ་འགྱུར་རོ།

།དེ་ཕྱིར་ཕྱོགས་དང་དུས་ཀྱིས་བསྡུས་པའི་སྣང་བ་ཐམས་ཅད་རང་སེམས་ཀྱི་སྣང་བ་ཙམ་མོ།

of conceptual thinking implanted in the all-ground consciousness since beginingless time. From the power of these [tendencies], it is merely mind as the all-ground consciousness and nothing other which manifests in the form of the appearances of environment, sense objects, and a body. All [appearances] are therefore only the appearance of mind. This is like the example of appearances in a dream.

[5,39] They [the proponents of the Mind Only School] also maintain that external objects have no existence other than [this all-ground] consciousness.

The ultimate dissection of coarse things, the basic components which are the two types of partless entities [atoms and instants], consequently cannot be established as having ultimate existence.

[5,40] Take for example the situation when partless atoms form a coarse thing. A single central atom is surrounded by six or ten atoms in the various directions. If those different atoms each have a part where they touch, [the central one] becomes endowed with parts. If they do not [touch the central one], then however many of the smallest atoms may be grouped together, it will not cause any further increase. An irreducible partless [atom] is therefore not established [as having ultimate existence]; it is merely an imputation.

[5,41] Take also the partless instant of time. If its previous and following partless [time entities] have different sides facing towards it, [this partless instant] becomes endowed with parts. And if they do not, there will not be any longer duration regardless of how many instants of the ultimately smallest time are added together, because they would each merely be one single instant.

[5,42] All appearances included within space and time are therefore only appearances of mind.

།འདི་ལྟ་བུའི་རྟེན་འབྲེལ་གྱི་སྣང་བ་འདི་ལ་གཞན་དབང་ཞེས་བྱ་སྟེ། རྟེན་འབྲེལ་གྱི་གཞན་དབང་གིས་སྣང་བ་ལས་རང་གི་ངོ་བོ་ཉིད་ཀྱིས་སྣང་བ་མིན་པའི་ཕྱིར་རོ།

།གཞན་དབང་གི་སྣང་བ་འདི་ལ་འདུས་བྱས་དང་འདུས་མ་བྱས་ཀྱི་ཆོས་སྣ་ཚོགས་ཀྱི་ངོ་བོ་དང་། གང་ཟག་ཏུ་སྒྲོ་བཏགས་པའི་བདག་གཉིས་ནི་ཀུན་བཏགས་སོ།

།ཀུན་བཏགས་པའི་སྤྱོད་ཡུལ་བདག་གཉིས་པོ་དེས་གཞན་དབང་གི་རྣམ་པར་ཤེས་པ་འདི་སྟོང་པ་ནི་ཡོངས་གྲུབ་སྟེ་འདིའི་ཆོས་ཉིད་དོ།

།དེ་ལྟ་ན་སྤྲོས་པ་ཀུན་གྱི་ཡུལ་མིན་པའི་གཟུང་འཛིན་གཉིས་སྟོང་གི་ཤེས་པ་རང་གསལ་ཙམ་ཞིག་དོན་དམ་པར་ཡོད་པར་འདོད་དོ།

།དབུ་མ་པས་ཇི་ལྟར་འདི་ནི་ཕྱི་དོན་མ་གྲུབ་པ་དེ་བཞིན་དེ་ལ་འཛིན་པའི་སེམས་ཀྱང་མི་འགྲུབ་ལ། དེ་གཉིས་ཀ་ཡང་རྟེན་འབྲེལ་གྱི་སྣང་བ་རང་གི་ངོ་བོ་ཉིད་མེད་པར་མཚུངས་ཤིང་སྤྲོས་པའི་ཡུལ་མིན་པའི་ཤེས་པ་ཞིག་རྫས་སུ་ཡོད་པའང་བཏགས་པ་ཙམ་སྟེ། གང་རང་གི་ངོ་བོ་ཡོད་ཅིང་དམིགས་སུ་རུང་བ་ཞིག་ཡིན་ཕན་ཆོད། དེའི་ངོ་བོ་ལ་བརྟགས་ན་བདེན་པར་གྲུབ་པ་ཙུང་ཟད་ཀྱང་མི་འགྲུབ་བོ།

།དེ་ལྟར་ཆོས་ཐམས་ཅད་རྟེན་ཅིང་འབྲེལ་བར་འབྱུང་བའི་དབང་གིས་སྣང་བ་བསླུ་མེད་དུ་ཤར་བ་ཙམ་ལས། རང་གི་ངོ་བོས་བདེན་པར་གྲུབ་པ་ཙུང་ཟད་ཀྱང་མེད་པས་སྟོང་པ་ཉིད་དུ་གནས་སོ།

།དེ་ལྟ་བུའི་སྟོང་པ་དང་རྟེན་འབྱུང་ལྡོག་པ་ཙམ་གྱི་སྒོ་ནས་ཐ་དད་དུ་བཞག་ཀྱང་། ངོ་བོ་ཐ་དད་དུ་མ་གྲུབ་པར་ཟུང་དུ་ཞུགས་པའི་དོན་སྤྲོས་བྲལ་སོ་སོ་རང་གིས་རིག་པར་བྱ་བ་ནི་ཆོས་ཀྱི་དབྱིངས་ཞེས་བྱ་ལ།

[5,43] Dependent [phenomena] are these interdependent appearances[23] because they appear through the dependency of connected [causes and conditions] and not through their own nature.

[5,44] Imagined [phenomena] are the two kinds of self-entity, the superimpositions on the dependent appearances as having identities of various conditioned and unconditioned phenomena and as having an individual [self-entity].

[5,45] The absolute is the nature of the dependent consciousness, the fact that it is empty of the two kinds of self-entity, the domains of the imagined.

[5,46] This being so, the proponents of the Mind Only School claim that the mere self-knowing consciousness — which is not the domain of [conceptual] constructs and which is devoid of both perceiver and the perceived — has ultimate existence.

[5,47] The followers of the Madhyamaka School maintain that just as an external object does not exist likewise the mind perceiving it also cannot be established [as truly existent].

[5,48] That is to say, both [object and mind] are alike in appearing due to [mutual] interdependence while they are devoid of a self-nature. Moreover, a substantially existent consciousness that is not the domain of constructs is but an imputation.

[5,49] Take a thing that has an individual identity and can be observed. When its identity is examined, it consequently cannot be established as having even the slightest true existence.

[5,50] All phenomena therefore merely occur as unfailing appearances through the power of dependent origination. Besides this, they are by nature devoid of even the slightest true existence and are therefore emptiness.

[5,51] Emptiness and dependent origination are merely described separately in terms of their opposites. Nevertheless, they are a unity devoid of separately existing identities that can be individually

དེ་ནི་རྟག་ཆད་དང་སྣང་སྟོང་སོགས་ཀྱི་མཐའ་དང་བྲལ་བ་དབུ་མའི་ལམ་གྱིས་རྟོགས་བྱ་ཡིན་ཞིང་རྟོགས་བྱ་དེའི་ངང་ན་སྟོང་རྟེན་འབྱུང་དོན་གཅིག་པར་གྲུབ་པའམ། ཐ་དད་དུ་མེད་པ་དང་། ཟུང་དུ་ཞུགས་པ་དང་། མཉམ་པར་གྲུབ་པ་ཞེས་འདོད་དོ།

།འདི་པས་གནས་ལུགས་ཇི་ལྟ་བ་བཞིན་གཏན་ལ་ཕེབས་པས་ན་གྲུབ་མཐའ་ཀུན་གྱི་ནང་ན་བླ་ན་མེད་པ་ཡིན་ནོ།

།བྱེ་མདོ་གཉིས་ཐེག་དམན་དང་། དབུ་སེམས་གཉིས་ཐེག་ཆེན་གྱི་གྲུབ་མཐའ་སྟེ། ཀུན་རྫོབ་དང་དོན་དམ་པའི་སེམས་རྣམ་པ་གཉིས་བསྐྱེད་ནས་ལམ་ལྔ་ས་བཅུར་ཐེག་པ་ཆེན་པོའི་དོན་ཉམས་སུ་བླངས་པས། འབྲས་བུ་མི་གནས་པའི་མྱང་འདས་སངས་རྒྱས་སུ་འགྲུབ་པར་འདོད་པ་མཚུངས་པའི་ཕྱིར་རོ།

།དབུ་སེམས་སོགས་ནང་གི་བྱེ་བྲག་ལས་འདོད་ཚུལ་མང་ཡང་། འདིར་སྤྱིའི་གནད་ཙམ་བརྗོད་པའོ།

།དེ་ལྟར་གྲུབ་པའི་མཐའ་གོང་ནས་གོང་དུ་ཇེ་བཟང་དུ་གྱུར་པའི་ཚུལ་ལ་བརྟེན་ཏེ། ཀུན་རྫོབ་དང་དོན་དམ་པའི་རང་བཞིན་ཕྱིན་ཅི་མ་ལོག་པར་རྟོགས་པ་ལས། ཆོས་ཐམས་ཅད་ཀྱི་གནས་དང་གནས་མ་ཡིན་པ་ལ་མཁས་པར་འགྱུར་རོ།

།གནས་དང་གནས་མིན་བཤད་པའི་སྐབས་སོ།

cognized. This absence of constructs is called *dharmadhatu* — the realm of phenomena.

This [dharmadhatu] is devoid of extremes such as being permanent or discontinued, apparent or empty, and is to be realized through the Middle Way, Madhyamaka.

Within the continuity of this [realm] to be realized, emptiness and dependent origination are one single fact, without separateness, united, and equal.

[5,52] Since this [Madhyamaka School] resolves the exact nature of things, it is unexcelled among all the schools of philosophy.

[5,53] Vaibhashika and Sautrantika are Hinayana schools. Madhyamaka and Mind Only are Mahayana schools because they are alike in accepting that after having aroused the two kinds of conventional and ultimate bodhimind, one practices the principles of the greater vehicle on the five paths and ten bhumis. Thereby one accomplishes the fruition of buddhahood, the non-dwelling nirvana.

[5,54] There are numerous systems of views among the various schools of Madhyamaka, Mind Only and the others, but here I have merely described the general points.

[5,55] Based on the manner in which these philosophical schools are successively more excellent, one realizes correctly the nature of what is conventional or ultimate. Therefrom one will become learned in what is correct or incorrect concerning all phenomena.

[5,56] This was the chapter on the correct and the incorrect. [27B:4]

དབང་པོ་ཉེར་གཉིས་ནི། མིག་གི་དབང་པོ་དང་། དེ་བཞིན་དུ་རྣ་བ་ནས་ཡིད་ཀྱི་དབང་པོའི་བར་དྲུག་གིས་རང་རང་གི་ཡུལ་འཛིན་པ་ལ་དབང་བྱེད།

སྲོག་གི་དབང་པོས་རིས་མཐུན་པར་གནས་པ་ལ་དབང་བྱེད།

ཕོ་དབང་དང་མོ་དབང་གིས་སོ་སོའི་རྟེན་ཅན་དུ་བྱེད་པ་དང་མངལ་ནས་སྐྱེ་བ་རྒྱུན་མི་འཆད་པ་ལ་དབང་བྱེད།

ཚོར་བ་བདེ་བའི་དབང་པོ། དེ་བཞིན་དུ། སྡུག་བསྔལ། ཡིད་བདེ། ཡིད་མི་བདེ། བཏང་སྙོམས་ཀྱི་དབང་པོ་ལྔས་རྣམ་སྨིན་གྱི་འབྲས་བུར་ལོངས་སྤྱོད་པ་ལ་དབང་བྱེད།

དད་བརྩོན་དྲན་པ་ཏིང་འཛིན་ཤེས་རབ་ཀྱི་དབང་པོ་ལྔས་འཇིག་རྟེན་པའི་དགེ་བའམ་དག་པ་ལ་དབང་བྱེད།

ཀུན་ཤེས་བྱེད་པ། ཀུན་ཤེས་པ། ཀུན་ཤེས་ལྡན་པའི་དབང་པོ་ཞེས་མཐོང་སྒོམ་མི་སློབ་པའི་རྒྱུད་ཀྱི་དད་སོགས་ཀྱིས་འཇིག་རྟེན་ལས་འདས་པའི་དག་པ་ལ་དབང་བྱེད་པས་དབང་པོ་ཞེས་བྱའོ།

6
The Faculties
Indriya

[6,1] There are twenty-two faculties:

[6,2] 1)-6) The six of the eye faculty, ear faculty and so forth until the mind faculty.[24] These six control the apprehending of their individual objects.

[6,3] 7) The life faculty controls the remaining in a similar class [of sentient beings].

[6,4] 8)-9) The male and female faculties form the respective physical supports [for being male or female] and control the unbroken continuity of births from a womb.

[6,5] 10)-14) The five faculties of the sensations of pleasure, pain, mental pleasure, mental pain, and of neutral sensation control the experiences of the fully ripened results [of karma].

[6,6] 15)-19) The five faculties of faith, diligence, recollection, concentration, and discrimination control the mundane virtues or the purity [of detachment].

[6,7] 20)-22) The faculties of 'making all understood', of 'understanding all,' and of 'having understood all' consist of faith and so forth in the stream-of-being of, [respectively, someone on the paths of] seeing, cultivation, and no-training. They control the supramundane purities [of noble beings].

[6,8] Faculties are therefore called [controlling] faculties.

།དེ་ལ་མིག་སོགས་དབང་པོ་དྲུག་ནི་སྔར་བཤད་པ་བཞིན་ལ། དེ་ལས་ཁྱད་པར་དུ་དབང་པོ་དྲུག་གི་ཟླས་ཕྱེ་བའི་ཡིད་དབང་ནི་ཡིད་ཞེས་སྐྱེད་པའི་རྟེན་ཙམ་ཡིན་ལ། འདིར་བཤད་པའི་ཡིད་དབང་ནི་རྟེན་དེ་ལས་སྐྱེས་པའི་ཡིད་ཞེས་ལ་ཡང་གོ་དགོས་སོ།

།དེ་དྲུག་གིས་རང་ཡུལ་འཛིན་ཚུལ་ནི། མིག་དང་རྣ་བའི་དབང་པོས་ཡུལ་མ་ཕྲད་པར་རྒྱང་ནས་འཛིན་ཅིང་། ཡུལ་རང་ལས་ཆེ་ཆུང་ངེས་མེད་འཛིན། སྣ་ལྕེ་ལུས་དབང་གསུམ་གྱིས་ཕྲད་ནས་འཛིན་ལ་ཡུལ་ཆེ་ཆུང་རང་དང་མཉམ་པ་འཛིན་ཏེ་འདི་དག་གི་ཡུལ་ཡུལ་ཅན་ཕན་ཚུན་ཐོགས་བཅས་ཀྱི་རིག་བྱ་ཅན་ཡིན་པའི་ཆ་ནས་ཕྲད་མ་ཕྲད་དཔྱད་དུ་ཡོད་དོ།

།ཡིད་དབང་ནི་རང་ཡུལ་ཆོས་ཁམས་ཙམ་དུ་མ་ཟད་ཆོས་ཐམས་ཅད་ཀྱི་ཡུལ་ཅན་ཡིན་པས། ངེས་ཡུལ་གང་དང་གང་བཟུང་བ་ལ་རིག་པའི་ཐ་སྙད་བྱེད་པ་སྟེ། བློ་དྭགས་ཆོག་གི་རིག་པ་ཞེས་ཀྱང་བརྗོད་དོ།

།དེའི་ཕྱིར་ཡུལ་དང་ཕྲད་མ་ཕྲད་དང་ཡུལ་རང་ལས་ཆེ་ཆུང་དཔྱད་དུ་མེད་དེ། ཞེས་པ་ལ་གཟུགས་མེད་པའི་ཕྱིར་རོ།

།འདུ་ཞེས་རྒྱ་ཆེ་ཆུང་སོགས་ནི་གཟུགས་ཆེ་ཆུང་མ་ཡིན་ཏེ་ཞེས་པ་ཉིད་ཀྱི་ཁྱབ་རྒྱ་ཆེ་ཆུང་ཡིན་ནོ།

ཕོ་དབང་དང་མོ་དབང་ནི། ལུས་དབང་གི་བྱེ་བྲག་མཐེ་བོང་ལྟ་བུ་དང་རྫའི་སྦུབས་ལྟ་བུ་ཕོ་མོ་འདུ་འཕྲད་ཀྱི་བདེ་བ་སྐྱོང་བ་སོགས་ཀྱི་རྟེན་བྱེད་པའོ།

[6,9] The six [sense] faculties of the eye and so forth have already been defined.

[6,10] The mind faculty taken from among the six [sense] faculties is merely the support for producing a mental cognition. Understand also that the mind faculty as mentioned here, also refers to a mental cognition produced from that support.

[6,11] Here is the manner in which these six [sense-faculties] apprehend their respective objects:

[6,12] The eye and ear faculties apprehend from a distance without meeting the object and apprehend [their objects] without any regularity as to whether the object is bigger or smaller than itself.

[6,13] The three faculties of the nose, tongue and body apprehend after meeting [with their object] and take hold of the object in a size equal to itself.

[6,14] Hence, in terms of these objects and 'object-possessors,' [the sense faculties], being mutually obstructive to touch, one can discern whether they meet [their object] or not.

[6,15] The mind faculty is not only the object-possessor, [subject], of just its own object, the element of mental objects, but [it is the object-possessor] of all phenomena. It apprehends and makes the names of contact with every object and is therefore also called nominal contact.

[6,16] It cannot be discerned whether its object is met or not met or whether the object is bigger or smaller that itself since consciousness has no [physical] form.

The size of a perception is not the size of the form but is the extent encompassed by the consciousness.

[6,17] The male and female faculties are particularities of the body faculty resembling the thumb and the hollow of a drum. They form the basis for experiencing the pleasure of contact between a male and a female.

།ཚོར་བ་ལྔ་དང་དད་སོགས་དང་སྲོག་ནི་སྔར་བཤད་པ་བཞིན་ནོ།

ཀུན་ཤེས་བྱེད་པ་མཐོང་ལམ་པའི་རྒྱུད་ཀྱི་དད་སོགས་ལྔ་དང་ཚོར་བ་བདེ་ཡིད་བདེ་བཏང་སྙོམས་གསུམ་དང་ཡིད་དབང་དང་དགུ་པོ་དེ་ལ་བརྗོད་པའོ།

།སྒོམ་ལམ་པའི་རྒྱུད་ཀྱི་དེ་དགུ་ལ་ཀུན་ཤེས་པའི་དབང་པོ། མི་སློབ་པའི་རྒྱུད་ཀྱི་དེ་དགུ་ལ་ཀུན་ཤེས་ལྡན་པའི་དབང་པོ་ཞེས་བྱའོ།

།དེ་ལྟར་དབང་པོ་ལ་གཟུགས་ཅན་བདུན་དང་། གཙོ་སེམས་ཅན་གཅིག་དང་། སེམས་བྱུང་བཅུ་དང་། ལྡན་མིན་འདུ་བྱེད་དུ་གཏོགས་པ་གཅིག་དང་། སེམས་སེམས་བྱུང་དགུ་ལས་བཏགས་པ་ཟག་མེད་ཀྱི་དབང་པོ་གསུམ་སྟེ་ཉེར་གཉིས་སོ།

།དབང་པོ་དེ་དག་གི་རབ་ཏུ་དབྱེ་བ་ལ། ཀུན་ཤེས་པར་བྱེད་པ་སོགས་གསུམ་ནི་ཟག་མེད་དོ།

།གཟུགས་ཅན་བདུན་དང་སྲོག་དང་སྡུག་བསྔལ་ཡིད་མི་བདེ་བཅས་བཅུ་པོ་སྒོམ་པས་སྤང་བྱ་ཡིན་པས་ཟག་བཅས་སོ། །དེའི་ལྷག་མ་ཚོར་བ་གསུམ་དང་དད་སོགས་ལྔ་ཡིད་དང་དགུ་ལ་ནི་ཟག་བཅས་ཟག་མེད་གཉིས་ཀྱི་ཆ་ཡོད་དོ།

།སྲོག་ནི་རྣམ་སྨིན་ལས་སྐྱེས་པ། དད་སོགས་ལྔ་ཀུན་ཤེས་སོགས་གསུམ་ཡིད་མི་བདེ་ནི་རྣམ་སྨིན་མིན་པའོ།

[6,18] The five kinds of sensation, the [five faculties of] faith and so forth, and the life [faculty] are as explained above.

[6,19] The [faculty] of 'making all understood' is described as being the nine [faculties] belonging to the stream-of-being of someone on the path of seeing. These are the five of faith and so forth, the three of the sensation of pleasure, mental pleasure, and indifference, and the mind faculty.

[6,20] The faculty of 'understanding all' is [comprised of the above] nine belonging to the stream-of-being of someone on the path of cultivation.

[6,21] The faculty of 'having understood all' is those nine belonging to the stream-of-being of someone on [the path of] no-training.

[6,22] Seven faculties have [physical] form. One is a 'main mind' [primary cognition]. Ten are mental states. One [the life faculty] belongs to nonconcurrent formations. The three undefiling faculties are named after the [main] mind and mental events. Thus there are twenty-two altogether.

[6,23] The presentation of the faculties:

[6,24] The three faculties of [the faculty of] 'making all understood' and so forth are undefiling.

[6,25] The seven with physical form, the life [faculty], the [sensations] of pain and mental pain, totaling ten, are defiling since they are to be abandoned by the [path of] cultivation.

[6,26] The nine remaining ones: the three [faculties] of the sensations [of pleasure, mental pleasure, and indifference], the five of faith and so forth, and the mind [faculty], have both aspects of being defiling [in an ordinary person] and undefiling [in a noble being].

[6,27] The life [faculty] is produced from [karmic] ripening. The five [faculties] of faith and so forth, the three of 'understanding all,' and mental pain,[25] are not produced from [karmic] ripening.

།དེ་ལ་ཡིད་མི་བདེ་ནི་རྟོག་པ་ཙམ་གྱིས་རང་འདོད་ཀྱིས་འཇུག་པས་རང་ཉིད་རྣམ་སྨིན་གྱི་འབྲས་བུ་མིན་ལ། དགེ་མི་དགེ་གང་རུང་དུ་ངེས་པས་རང་གིས་རྣམ་སྨིན་གྱི་འབྲས་བུ་འབྱིན་པ་དང་བཅས་པའོ་ཞེས་བྱེ་སྨྲས་འདོད་ཀྱང་། རྣམ་སྨིན་གྱི་ཆ་ལུང་མ་བསྟན་ཡང་ཡོད་དགོས་པར་མདོན་ནོ་སྙམ། འདི་དག་གི་ཞིབ་ཆ་གཞན་དུ་བཤད་པར་བྱའོ།

།གོང་གི་ལྷག་མ་བཅུ་གཉིས་ལས། གཟུགས་ཅན་བདུན་རྣམ་སྨིན་ལས་བྱུང་བ་དང་། རྒྱས་བྱུང་རྣམས་རྣམ་སྨིན་མིན་ཀྱང་ཟེར། ཡིད་དང་ཚོར་བ་གཞན་བཞི་ལ་ནི་དགེ་མི་དགེ་ལུང་མ་བསྟན་གསུམ་ཡོད་པས། དགེ་མི་དགེ་ཟག་བཅས་རྣམས་རྣམ་སྨིན་དང་བཅས་པ་དང་། ལུང་མ་བསྟན་རྣམས་ལ་རྣམ་སྨིན་མེད་པའོ། །དད་སོགས་ལྔ་ཟག་བཅས་རྣམ་སྨིན་དང་བཅས་པ། ཟག་མེད་ཀྱི་ཡིད་དང་ཚོར་བ་དད་སོགས་ལྔ་པོ་རྣམས་ལ་རྣམ་སྨིན་མེད་དོ། །རྣམ་སྨིན་ནི་འཁོར་བའི་རྣམ་སྨིན་ལ་འཛིན་དགོས་སོ།

།དད་སོགས་ལྔ་དང་ཀུན་ཤེས་སོགས་གསུམ་དགེ་བའོ། །ཡིད་དང་ཚོར་བ་བདེ་སོགས་ལ་དགེ་མི་དགེ་ལུང་མ་བསྟན་གསུམ་ཡོད་དོ། །གཟུགས་ཅན་བདུན་དང་སྲོག་དབང་དང་བརྒྱད་ནི་ལུང་མ་བསྟན་ནོ།

།དྲི་མེད་གསུམ་མ་གཏོགས་པ་གཞན་བཅུ་དགུ་པོ་ཐམས་ཅད་འདོད་པར་གཏོགས་པ་ན་ཡོད། དེ་ལས་ཕོ་མོའི་དབང་པོ་དང་སྡུག་བསྔལ་གཉིས་མ་གཏོགས་པ་གཞན་གཟུགས་ཁམས་ན་ཡང་ཡོད།

[6,28] The Vaibhashikas maintain that the [sensation of] mental pain among these [faculties] is not itself the result of ripening because of being an involvement through personal desire due to mere conceptualization. Since it can be determined as either virtuous or unvirtuous, it yields its own ripened result. Nevertheless, I think it is evident that there should also be a neutral aspect of the ripening [of past actions]. The details of this will be explained elsewhere.

[6,29] Among the remaining twelve of the above, the seven having form result from [karmic] ripening. It is also said that development is not a [karmic] ripening.

[6,30] The mind faculty and the other four sensations[26] have three [aspects] virtuous, unvirtuous, and neutral. Defiling virtue and nonvirtue therefore have [karmic] ripening, while the neutral has no ripening.[27]

[6,31] The [defiling] five faculties of faith and so forth have ripening. The undefiling mind faculty, sensations, and [the undefiling] five of faith and so forth all have no ripening. Understand that ripening here means samsaric ripening.

[6,32] The five faculties of faith and so forth and the three of 'understanding all' and so forth are virtuous.

[6,33] The mind [faculty] and sensation of pleasure and so forth have the three aspects of being virtuous, unvirtuous, and neutral.

[6,34] The eight faculties consisting of the seven having form and the life faculty are neutral.

[6,35] Except for the three flawless [faculties], the other nineteen can all be present in the [beings] belonging to the Desire [Realm].

[6,36] Among them, except for the male and female faculties and the two kinds of [sensation] of pain [and mental pain], the other [faculties] can be present in the [sentient beings] in the Form Realms.

གཟུགས་ཅན་བདུན་དང་བཏང་སྙོམས་མིན་པའི་ཚོར་བ་གཞན་བཞི་མ་གཏོགས་པའི་ལྷག་མ་རྣམས་གཟུགས་མེད་ན་ཡོད། ཟག་མེད་གསུམ་ནི་ཁམས་གསུམ་པའི་ཆོས་སུ་གཏོགས་པ་མིན་ཡང་། ཁམས་གསུམ་པའི་རྒྱུད་ལ་མི་འབྱུང་བ་མ་ཡིན་ནོ།

།ཡིད་དང་ཚོར་བ་བདེ་ཡིད་བདེ་བཏང་སྙོམ་བཞི་ལ་མཐོང་སྤང་སྒོམ་སྤང་སྤང་བྱ་མིན་པ་གསུམ་ཡོད། ཡིད་མི་བདེ་ནི་མཐོང་སྒོམ་གཉིས་ཀྱིས་སྤང་བྱའོ། །གོང་བཤད་ལྟར་གཟུགས་ཅན་བདུན་སོགས་བཅུ་ནི་སྒོམ་པས་སྤང་བྱའོ། །དད་སོགས་ལྔ་ཟག་བཅས་སྒོམ་སྤང་། ཟག་མེད་སྤང་བྱ་མིན་ནོ། དྲི་མེད་ཀྱི་དབང་པོ་གསུམ་སྤང་བྱ་མིན་ནོ།

།དབང་པོ་དེ་དག་སྐྱེད་ཚུལ་ནི།

འདོད་ཁམས་སུ་མངལ་སྐྱེས་སོགས་ཀྱི་དང་པོར་རྣམ་སྨིན་གྱི་དབང་པོ་ལུས་སྲོག་གཉིས་སྐྱེད། རྫུས་སྐྱེས་མཚན་མེད་བསྐལ་པ་དང་པོའི་མི་རྣམས་ལྟ་བུས་མིག་སོགས་ལྔ་སྲོག་དང་དྲུག་ཅིག་ཆར་སྐྱེད།

མཚན་གཅིག་པ་རྫུས་སྐྱེས་འདོད་ལྷ་རྣམས་ལྟ་བུས་སྔ་མ་དྲུག་གི་སྟེང་དུ་ཕོ་མོའི་དབང་པོ་གང་རུང་སྟེ་བདུན་སྐྱེད།

[6,37] Except for the seven having form and the four sensations other than indifference, the remaining ones can all be present in the Formless [Realms].[28]

[6,38] Although the three undefiling [faculties] do not belong under the phenomena of the three realms, that does not mean that they cannot occur within the stream-of-being of someone in the three realms.

[6,39] The four faculties consisting of the mind faculty, the sensations of pleasure, mental pleasure and indifference have three [aspects]: to be discarded [through the path of] seeing, to be discarded [through] cultivation, and not to be discarded.

[6,40] Mental pain is to be discarded through both [the paths of] seeing and cultivation.

[6,41] As explained above, the ten faculties consisting of the seven having form and so on [plus life, pain and mental pain] are to be discarded by [the path of] cultivation. The five defiling faculties consisting of faith and so forth are discarded through cultivation, while the undefiling are not to be discarded. The three flawless faculties are not to be discarded.

[6,42] The way in which these faculties are obtained:

[6,43] To begin with, the ones who are womb-born in the Desire Realms obtain the two [karmically] ripened faculties of body and life.

[6,44] The genderless instantaneously-born, as for instance human beings in the first aeon, obtain simultaneously the six faculties consisting of the five [faculties] of eye and so forth and the life [faculty].

[6,45] The single-gender instantaneously-born, such as the desire gods, obtain in addition to the former six either the male or the female faculty, totaling seven.

རྫུས་སྐྱེས་མཚན་གཉིས་པ་ངན་སོང་ལ་སྲིད་པས་དེ་ལྟ་ན་བརྒྱད་རྙེད་དོ།

།གཟུགས་ཁམས་ནས་དེའི་མིག་སོགས་ལྔ་སྲོག་དང་དྲུག་རྙེད་དོ། གཟུགས་མེད་ན་སྲོག་དབང་གཅིག་པུ་གསར་དུ་རྙེད་དོ།

།ཡང་གཟུགས་མེད་དུ་འཆི་བ་ན་སྲོག་དང་ཡིད་དང་བཏང་སྙོམས་ཀྱི་དབང་པོ་གསུམ་ཅིག་ཆར་དུ་འགག་གོ། །གཟུགས་ཁམས་ན་དེ་གསུམ་དང་མིག་སོགས་ལྔ་སྟེ་བརྒྱད་དུས་གཅིག་འགག་གོ། །རྫུས་སྐྱེས་རྣམས་ཅིག་ཆར་འཆི་བས་མཚན་གཉིས་པ་ལ་སྔ་མ་བརྒྱད་ལ་མཚན་གཉིས་བསྣན་པས་བཅུ་འགག་གོ། །མཚན་གཅིག་ལ་དགུ་དང་། མཚན་མེད་ལ་བརྒྱད་དོ། །མངལ་སྐྱེས་སོགས་རིམ་གྱིས་འཆི་བ་དག་ལ་ལུས་ཡིད་སྲོག་བཏང་སྙོམས་བཞི་ཅིག་ཆར་འགག་གོ། དེ་རྣམས་ནི་མ་བསྒྲིབ་ལུང་མ་བསྟན་དང་ཉོན་མོངས་པས་འཆི་སེམས་ཀྱི་དབང་དུ་བྱས་ཀྱི། དགེ་སེམས་སྐྱེས་ཐོབ་ལ་གནས་ཏེ་འཆི་བ་ལ་ཐམས་ཅད་དུ་དད་སོགས་ལྔ་བསྣན་པས་གཟུགས་མེད་དུ་བརྒྱད་འགག་པ་སོགས་སོ།

།དབང་པོ་གང་གིས་རྒྱུན་ཞུགས་སོགས་འབྲས་བུ་བཞི་ཐོབ་ཚུལ་དཔྱད་ན།

རྒྱུན་ཞུགས་དང་དགྲ་བཅོམ་པའི་འབྲས་བུ་ནི།

ཡིད་དང་དད་སོགས་ལྔ་སྟེ་དྲུག་གི་སྟེང་དུ། རྒྱུན་ཞུགས་ནི་འདོད་ཁམས་ལ་ཆགས་བཅས་ཡིན་པས་མི་ལྡོགས་མེད་ཀྱི་བཏང་སྙོམས་དང་། མཐོང་ལམ་སྐད་ཅིག་བཅོ་ལྔ་པར་ཀུན་ཤེས་བྱེད་པ་དང་བཅུ་དྲུག་པར་ཀུན་ཤེས་ཏེ་དགུས་ཐོབ་བོ།

[6,46] The double-gender instantaneously-born who are possible in the lower realms thus obtain eight.

[6,47] In the Form Realms one obtains the six faculties consisting of the five of eye and so forth and the life [faculty].[29]

[6,48] In the Formless [Realms] one only obtains anew the life faculty.

[6,49] When dying in the Formless [Realms] the three faculties of life, mind, and indifferent [sensation] cease simultaneously.

[6,50] In the Form Realms, the eight faculties consisting of those three and the five of eye and so forth cease simultaneously.

[6,51] [In the Desire Realms] the instantaneously-born dies all at once. For the double-gender ten [faculties] cease by adding the two genders to the previous eight. For the single-gendered nine cease; and for the genderless eight [cease].

[6,52] For the womb-born and so forth [egg or heat-born], who die gradually, the four faculties of body, mind, life, and indifferent [sensation] cease simultaneously.

[6,53] All these cases [of ceasing of faculties] are mentioned in terms of a dying mind that is not obscuring, undetermined or disturbed. For the beings who die abiding in a virtuous mentality acquired by birth, eight [faculties] cease for someone in the Formless [Realms] and so on by adding the five [faculties] of faith and so forth.

[6,54] Here follows an examination of which faculties cause the four results such as stream-enterer to be obtained.

[6,55] The results of a stream-enterer and arhat:

[6,56] In addition to the six consisting of the mind [faculty] and the five of faith and so forth, the stream-enterer, because of being attached to the Desire Realms, obtains the [faculty of] the indifferent [sensation] of the capable stage. He likewise obtains the [faculty of] 'making all understood' in the fifteenth moment of

དགྲ་བཅོམ་པ་བསམ་གཏན་དང་པོ་གཉིས་ཀྱི་དངོས་གཞིར་བརྟེན་ན་དེ་གཉིས་ཀྱི་ཡིད་བདེ་དང་། གསུམ་པ་ལ་བརྟེན་ན་བདེ་བ། དེ་གསུམ་མ་ཡིན་པའི་ས་གང་ལ་བརྟེན་ཀྱང་བཏང་སྙོམས་ཏེ། དེ་གསུམ་གང་རུང་དང་། བར་ཆད་མེད་ལམ་རྗོར་ཏིང་ཀུན་ཞེས་པ་དང་། རྣམ་གྲོལ་ལམ་ཀུན་ཞེས་ལྡན་པ་སྡེ་དགུས་ཐོབ་བོ།

།ཕྱིར་འོང་ཕྱིར་མི་འོང་གཉིས་ནི།

ཡིད་དང་དད་སོགས་དྲུག་གི་སྡེང་དུ། ཕྱིར་འོང་རིམ་གྱིས་པ་འཇིག་རྟེན་པའི་ལམ་གྱིས་འབྲས་བུ་ཐོབ་པར་བྱེད་ན་མི་ལྕོགས་མེད་པའི་བཏང་སྙོམས་དང་བདུན། འདས་ལམ་གྱིས་ཐོབ་ན་དེའི་དད་སོགས་ལྔ་ལ་ཀུན་ཞེས་ཀྱི་མིང་ཐོབ་པས་དེ་དང་བརྒྱད་ཀྱིས་སོ།

།འཇིག་རྟེན་པའི་ལམ་གྱི་ཆགས་བྲལ་སྔོན་སོང་གིས་མཐོང་ལམ་དུ་ཕྱིར་འོང་རང་འབྲས་ཐོབ་པ་ལ་བརྒྱད་པོའི་སྡེང་དུ་ཀུན་ཞེས་བྱེད་དང་དགུའོ།

།ཕྱིར་མི་འོང་དབང་བརྟུལ་གྱིས་འཇིག་རྟེན་པའི་ལམ་གྱིས་མཐར་གྱིས་ཐོབ་ན། དང་པོའི་དངོས་གཞིའི་ཡིད་བདེ་རྣམ་གྲོལ་དགུ་པའི་ཚེ་མངོན་དུ་བྱེད་མི་ནུས་པས་མི་ལྕོགས་མེད་ཀྱི་བཏང་སྙོམས་དང་བདུན་ནོ།

།ཡང་མཐར་གྱིས་པ་དབང་རྟུལ་འདས་ལམ་གྱིས་ཐོབ་ན་དེ་སྡེང་ཀུན་ཞེས་དང་བརྒྱད།

the path of seeing, and the [faculty of] 'understanding all' in the sixteenth [moment], totaling nine.

[6,57] The arhat, when adhering to the main part of the first and second dhyanas, obtains [the faculty of] the mental pleasure of those two. Additionally he obtains the [faculty of] pleasure when adhering to the third [dhyana]. Adhering to any level that is neither of these three, he obtains the [faculty of] indifferent [sensation]. On either of these three or in the vajra-like samadhi of the path without impediment he obtains the 'understanding all,' and on the path of liberation [he obtains] the [faculty of] 'having understood all'. Thus, nine in all.

[6,58] The [results of] the once-returner and the non-returner:

When achieving his result through the mundane path, the gradual once-returner, in addition to the six consisting of [the faculties of] mind and the five of faith and so forth, obtains seven by adding the indifferent [sensation of] the capable stage. When achieving through the supramundane path, he obtains the name of 'understanding all' in regard to the five of faith and so forth of that path, totaling eight.

[6,59] Through the mundane path, the one who is already detached obtains, in order to achieve his result of non-returner, the [faculty of] 'making all understood' in addition to the eight, thus nine in all.

[6,60] The dull non-returner gradually achieves through the mundane path. He has seven faculties when adding the indifference of the capable stage because of being unable to realize the [sensation of] pleasure of the main part of the first [dhyana] at the time of the nine aspects of liberation.[30]

[6,61] When the dull gradual type achieves through the supramundane path, he obtains eight faculties with the additional 'understanding all'.

གལ་ཏེ་དབང་རྣོན་འཇིག་རྟེན་པའི་ལམ་གྱིས་ཀྱང་དངོས་གཞིའི་ཡིད་བདེ་མངོན་དུ་བྱེད་ནུས་ན་ཡང་དེ་དང་བརྒྱད་དོ།

།དབང་རྣོན་འདས་ལམ་གྱིས་ཐོབ་ན་བཏང་སྙོམས་ཡིད་བདེ་གཉིས་དང་བར་ཆད་མེད་ལམ་གྱི་ཚེ་ཀུན་ཤེས་དང་དགུས་ཐོབ་བོ།

།ཡང་ཆགས་བྲལ་སྔོན་སོང་གིས་རང་འབྲས་ཐོབ་ན། ཚོར་བ་གསུམ་གང་རུང་དང་། ཀུན་ཤེས་བྱེད་པ་དང་། ཀུན་ཤེས་པ་དང་དགུས་ཐོབ་བོ།

།ལྡན་ཚུལ་ནི། བཏང་སྙོམས་དང་ཡིད་དང་སྲོག་གང་རུང་དང་ལྡན་ན། གསུམ་ཀ་ངེས་པར་ལྡན་ནོ།

།བདེ་བ་དང་ལུས་དབང་ལྡན་ན། སྔར་གྱི་གསུམ་སྟེ་རང་རང་དང་བཞི་ལྡན་ནོ།

།མིག་སོགས་ལྡན་ན་གོང་གི་གསུམ་དང་ལུས་དང་རང་དང་ལྔ་ལྡན་ནོ།

།ཡིད་བདེ་དང་ལྡན་ན་གོང་གསུམ་ལུས་དང་རང་བཅས་ལྔ་ལྡན་ནོ། སྡུག་བསྔལ་ལྡན་པ་ལ་གོང་གི་གསུམ་དང་ལུས་དང་བདེ་ཡིད་བདེ་རང་བཅས་བདུན་ལྡན་ནོ།

།ཕོ་མོའི་དབང་པོ་གང་རུང་དང་ལྡན་པ་ལ་གོང་གི་བདུན་སྟེང་རང་དང་བརྒྱད་ལྡན་ནོ།

།ཡིད་མི་བདེ་བ་ལ་ཡང་གོང་གི་བདུན་སྟེང་རང་བསྣན་ཏེ་བརྒྱད།

།དད་སོགས་ལྔ་ལ་གོང་གསུམ་སྟེང་ལྔ་པོ་བསྣན་ཏེ་བརྒྱད་དོ།

[6,62] When the sharp [gradual type] through the mundane path is able to realize the mental pleasure of the main part, he also obtains eight [faculties].

[6,63] When the sharp type achieves through the supramundane path he obtains [the faculties of] both the [sensations of] indifference and mental pleasure and of the 'understanding all' at the time of the path without impediment, thus nine in all.

[6,64] Moreover, when the already detached type achieves his respective result [of non-return], he obtains it by means of the nine faculties of either of the three sensations, the 'making all understood' and the 'understanding all.'

[6,65] The way in which someone possesses [the faculties]:

[6,66] When possessing either indifference, mind, or life, one definitely possesses all three.

[6,67] When possessing the [sensation of] pleasure or body, one possesses four: that one in addition to the former three.

[6,68] When possessing the eye [faculty] etc., one possesses five: that [faculty] itself, the former three, and the body [faculty].

[6,69] When possessing the [faculty of the sensation of] mental pleasure, one possesses five: three above, the body and [that faculty] itself.

[6,70] Those who possess the [faculty of the sensation of] pain, will possess seven: the above three, the body, pleasure and mental pleasure, and [that faculty] itself.

[6,71] When possessing either the male or female faculty, one possesses eight: the above seven and itself.

[6,72] When [having] the [faculty of] mental pain, one has eight when adding the above seven.

[6,73] When having the five of faith and so forth, one has eight when adding the above three.

།ཀུན་ཤེས་ལྡན་པའི་དབང་པོ་ལྡན་ན། ཟག་མེད་དགུ་དང་སྲོག་དང་རང་བཅས་བཅུ་གཅིག་ལྡན་ནོ།

ཀུན་ཤེས་བྱེད་པ་འདོད་པའི་རྟེན་ཅན་ཡིན་པས་གོང་གི་བཅུ་གཅིག་པོའི་སྟེང་དུ་ལུས་དང་སྡུག་བསྔལ་བསྣན་པས་བཅུ་གསུམ་དང་ལྡན་ནོ།

།མང་ལྡན་ཉུང་ལྡན་གྱི་ཁྱད་པར་ནི། དགེ་རྩ་མེད་པའི་ནང་ན་དབང་པོ་ཉུང་བ་དང་ལྡན་པ་དག་ལུས་དང་ཚོར་བ་ལྔ་སྲོག་དང་ཡིད་བཅས་བརྒྱད་དང་ལྡན་ནོ།

།གཟུགས་མེད་ཀྱི་བྱིས་པ་ཡང་། བཏང་སྙོམས་སྲོག་ཡིད་གསུམ་དང་དད་སོགས་ལྔ་སྟེ་བརྒྱད་དང་ལྡན་ནོ།

།མང་པོར་ལྡན་པ་ལ་སོ་སྐྱེ་མཚན་གཉིས་པ་ལ་དྲི་མེད་གསུམ་མ་གཏོགས་པ་བཅུ་དགུ་ལྡན་ནོ།

།ཡང་ན་འཕགས་པ་ཆགས་བཅས་མཚན་གཅིག་པ་ལ་དྲི་མེད་ཕྱི་མ་གཉིས་མ་གཏོགས་པའི་བཅུ་དགུ་ལྡན་པ་ཤེས་པར་བྱའོ།

།དབང་པོའི་སྐབས་སོ།

[6,74] When having the faculty of 'having understood all', one possesses eleven: the nine undefiling, the life [faculty] and itself.[31]

[6,75] The [faculty of] 'making all understood' has a bodily support in the case of someone in the Desire [Realms]. Therefore, one possesses thirteen by adding the [faculties of] body and of [the sensation of] pain to the above eleven.

[6,76] The different ways of possessing the most or the fewest:

[6,77] Among the beings without roots of virtue, those who possess the fewest faculties possess eight: the body, five sensations, life, and mind.

[6,78] Immature beings of the Formless [Realms] also possess eight: the three of indifference, life, and mind, and the five of faith and so forth.

[6,79] As to those who possess the most, it should be understood that a double-gendered ordinary person can, excepting the three flawless ones, possess nineteen. Or, a noble single-gendered with attachment can possess nineteen excepting the last two flawless [faculties].

[6,80] This was the chapter on the faculties.

།དུས་ཞེས་བྱ་བ་ནི་གསུམ་སྟེ།

རྒྱུ་འབྲས་གཉིས་ཀ་སྐྱིད་ཟིན་པ་ལ་འདས་པའི་དུས་ཞེས་སྔོན་བྱུང་ཟིན་ནས་འགགས་པའོ། །རྒྱུ་སྐྱིད་ལ་འབྲས་བུ་སྐྱིད་མ་ཟིན་པ་ད་ལྟ་བའི་དུས་སོ། །རྒྱུ་ཡོད་ཀྱང་ད་ལྟ་རྒྱུ་མ་ཚང་བས་འབྲས་བུ་ཡང་སྐྱིད་དུ་མེད་པ་ལ། མ་འོང་པའི་དུས་ཞེས་བྱ་སྟེ།

དེ་ལྟར་དུས་གསུམ་པོ་དག་ནི་དངོས་པོ་རྣམས་ཀྱི་རྒྱུ་འབྲས་ཀྱི་སྣང་བ་ལ་བརྟེན་ནས་རྣམ་བཞག་གི་སྒོ་ནས་བཏགས་པའོ།

།དུས་གསུམ་གྱིས་བསྡུས་པའི་དུས་དེ་དག་ཡུན་རིང་ཐུང་གི་ཚད་ཀྱི་སྒོ་ནས་འདི་དང་འདི་ལྟ་བུའོ་ཞེས་ཤེས་པར་བྱེད་པ་ལ། དེའི་ཡུན་ཞེས་པ་འདས་ད་ལྟ་མ་འོངས་པའི་ཚུལ་གྱིས་སྐད་ཅིག་མའི་ཕྲེང་བ་རིམ་གྱིས་འབྱུང་བའི་ཚུལ་བཤད་ན། དུས་ཀྱི་མཐར་ཤིན་ཏུ་ཕྲ་བ་སྔ་ཕྱིའི་ཆ་དབྱེར་མེད་པ་ལ་དུས་མཐའི་སྐད་ཅིག་མ་ཞེས་བྱའོ།

།དུས་མཐའི་སྐད་ཅིག་མ་བརྒྱ་ཉི་ཤུ་ལ་དེ་ཡི་སྐད་ཅིག་གཅིག། དེའི་སྐད་ཅིག་དྲུག་ཅུ་ལ་ཐང་ཅིག། ཐང་ཅིག་སུམ་ཅུ་ལ་ཡུད་ཙམ་གཅིག། ཡུད་ཙམ་སུམ་ཅུ་ལ་ཉིན་ཞག་གཅིག། ཉིན་ཞག་སུམ་ཅུ་ར་ཟླ་བ་གཅིག། ཟླ་བ་བཅུ་གཉིས་ལ་ལོ་གཅིག། ཅེས་བྱའོ།

7
TIME

[7,1] Time has three aspects.

[7,2] The past [of a certain thing] is the completed enacting of both cause and effect. It is the completion and cessation of what has previously happened. Present means that the cause has been enacted but not the effect. Future is the incompleteness of causes, although a cause may be present, while an effect has not been enacted.

[7,3] In this way, these three times are imputed by systems in terms of the appearance of the cause and effect of things.

[7,4] These three times make one understand that [a thing lasts] for such and such [a duration] by means of measures of long and short durations.

[7,5] Concerning the duration of something, when we explain gradual occurrence of a string of moments in the manner of past, present, and future, the most subtle and ultimately smallest time where former and following parts are indivisible is called the ultimately smallest instant of time [according to the Abhidharma].

One hundred and twenty such ultimately smallest instants of time are one 'moment'. Sixty such moments are 'one minute'. Thirty such minutes are one period. Thirty such periods are one day [and night]. Thirty days are one month and twelve months are one year. So it has been taught.

།སྐར་རྩིས་ཀྱི་གཞུང་ནས་སྐྱེས་བུ་དར་མ་ཁམས་སྙོམས་པའི་དབུགས་འབྱིན་རྔུབ་རྣལ་མ་ཟུང་རེ་གཅིག་ཏུ་བརྩིས་པ་ལ་དབུགས་གཅིག་ཞེས་བྱ། དབུགས་དྲུག་ལ་ཆུ་སྲང་གཅིག། ཆུ་སྲང་དྲུག་ཅུ་ལ་ཆུ་ཚོད་གཅིག། ཆུ་ཚོད་དྲུག་ཅུ་ལ་ཞག་གཅིག་ཏུ་བཤད་དོ།

།དེ་གཉིས་བསྡུན་ཏེ་གོ་བདེར་བརྗོད་ན། ཞག་གཅིག་ལ་དུས་མཐའི་སྐད་ཅིག་མ་ས་ཡ་དྲུག་དང་འབུམ་ཕྲག་བཞི་ཁྲི་བརྒྱད་ཡོད་དོ། །དབུགས་ཉི་ཁྲི་ཆིག་སྟོང་དྲུག་བརྒྱ་ཡོད། དབུགས་རེའི་ཡུན་ལ་དུས་མཐའི་སྐད་ཅིག་མ་སུམ་བརྒྱ་ཡོད་དོ།

།དབུགས་འབྱིན་རྔུབ་རེའི་ཡུན་ལ་སྐྱེས་བུ་ནད་མེད་ཐ་མལ་པའི་རྩ་ལན་ལྔ་འཕར་བ་ཡིན་པས། ཡུད་ཙམ་གཅིག་ལ་ཆུ་ཚོད་གཉིས་ཡོད་ཆུ་སྲང་ལྟར་ན་བརྒྱ་དང་ཉི་ཤུ་ཡོད། ཐང་གཅིག་རེ་ནི་ཆུ་སྲང་བཞིའི་ཡུན་ནོ། །དེའི་སྐད་ཅིག་མའི་ཡུན་ནི་རྩ་ལན་གཉིས་འཕར་ཡུན་ནོ།

།དེ་ལྟར་བརྩིས་ན་རྩ་རེ་རེ་འཕར་ཡུན་དང་སེ་གོལ་རན་པར་གཏོགས་པ་དུས་མཉམ་པར་བྱུས་ཏེ།

དེའི་ཡུན་ལ་ཨོ་མང་གི་འདབ་མ་དྲུག་ཅུ་ཐམ་པ་བརྩེགས་པ་ཁབ་ཀྱིས་ཕུག་པས་འདབ་མ་རེ་རེ་འབུག་པའི་ཡུན་ནི་དུས་མཐའི་སྐད་ཅིག་མའི་ཚད་དུ་ཤེས་པར་བྱ་སྟེ། འདབ་མ་རྣམས་རིམ་ཅན་དུ་འབུག་པ་ལས་ཅིག་ཆར་འབུག་མི་སྲིད་པས་རེ་རེ་འབུག་པའི་ཡུན་དེ་ལས་རྗེས་སུ་དཔག་ནས་ཤེས་པ་ཡིན་ནོ། །དྲུག་ཅུ་རྩ་བཞི་དང་རྩ་ལྟར་གསུང་པ་བརྩིས་ན་གཞུང་དང་མི་འགྲིགས་པས་དགོངས་པ་བརྟག་པར་བྱའོ། །སྐད་ཅིག་མ་འདི་ལ་དུས་མཐའི་སྐད་ཅིག་དང་། བྱ་རྫོགས་ཀྱི་སྐད་ཅིག་མ་གཉིས་ཡོད་པའི། དང་པོ་གོང་དུ་བཤད་པ་དུས་ཀྱི་ཐུང་མཐའོ།

།གཉིས་པ་བྱ་བ་གང་ཡིན་པ་དེ་མགོ་བརྩམ་ནས་ཡོངས་སུ་རྫོགས་པའི་བར་གྱི་ཡུན་ལ་འཇོག་པས་བྱ་བ་ལ་ལྟོས་ནས་རིང་ཐུང་མ་ངེས་པ་སྣ་ཚོགས་ཡོད་དེ།

[7,6] The root texts of astrology[32] [and Abhidharma] explain that, counted as one, the pair of a regular inhalation and exhalation of breath of an adult in good health is called one breath. Six such breaths are one water-measure. Sixty such water-measures are one half-period and sixty such half-periods are one day [and night].[33]

[7,7] When explaining these in an easily understood way by correlating them, there are in one day six million four hundred eighty thousand ultimately smallest instants and there are twenty-one thousand six hundred breaths. In the duration of each breath there are three hundred ultimately smallest instants.

[7,8] In the duration of each inhalation and exhalation of breath, the pulse of an ordinary person in good health beats five times. One period, that is two half-periods, has one hundred and twelve water-measures. Each 'minute' is the duration of four water-measures. The duration of one 'moment' is the time it takes the pulse to beat two times.

[7,9] When calculating in this way, the duration of each pulse beat and a regular finger-snap are of equal length of time.

[7,10] The measure of the ultimately smallest instant of time is known as the timespan it takes to pierce each leaf when piercing a needle through sixty piled *shomang* leaves. The petals are all pierced gradually since it is not possible to pierce them simultaneously. The duration it takes to pierce each is therefore understood through inference. If one were to calculate with the sometimes mentioned sixty-four or five [leaves] there comes disagreement with the root texts, so one should examine the intent of that.

[7,11] There are two kinds of moments: the ultimately smallest instant of time and the 'moment of completing an act'. The first is the shortest, ultimately smallest time explained above. The second is defined as the duration from the beginning of any action until it is fully completed. So, dependent on the action, it has an infinite number of lengths of duration.

ཐུང་བ་སེ་གོལ་ཙམ་གཏོགས་པའི་བྱ་བ་རྫོགས་པ་ལ་ཡང་དེའི་མིང་ཐོབ་ཅིང་། རིང་བ་སངས་རྒྱས་ཀྱིས་དང་པོར་ཐུགས་བསྐྱེད་ནས་མཐར་བླ་མེད་བྱང་ཆུབ་མངོན་དུ་མཛད་པའི་བར་ལ་ཡང་བྱ་བ་རྫོགས་པའི་སྐད་ཅིག་གཅིག་ཏུ་འདོད་རུང་བ་ཡིན་ནོ།

།དེ་ལྟར་དངོས་པོ་རྣམས་ཀྱི་ཡུན་ལ་སྐྱེས་བུའི་འདོད་པའི་དབང་གིས་དུས་སུ་བརྡ་འདོགས་པའི་ཕྱིར། རེས་ད་ལྟ་རང་དུས་སུ་ཡོད་པ་ཁོ་ན་ད་ལྟ་བ། དེའི་སྔར་བྱུང་ཐམས་ཅད་འདས་པ། རྗེས་སུ་འོང་འགྱུར་མ་འོངས་པར་བརྗོད་དེ་སྐད་ཅིག་ལ་དཔྱད་པའི་དབང་དུ་བྱས་པའོ།

།རེས་བསྐལ་པ་འདི་ཆགས་ནས་མ་སྟོང་གི་བར་ལ་ད་ལྟ་བར་བྱེད་ཅིང་། དེའི་སྔ་ཕྱིར་བྱུང་བ་འདས་མ་འོངས་སུ་བྱེད་དོ། །དེ་ནི་འདོགས་ཡུལ་གྱི་དབང་གིས་དུས་ཀྱི་རྒྱུན་བློས་སྦྱོམས་སྟེ་ཐ་སྙད་དེ་ལྟ་བུ་ཡང་བྱེད་རུང་བ་ཡིན་ནོ།

།དེའི་ཕྱིར་འཇིག་རྟེན་ལ་བརྟེན་ཏེ། བསྐལ་པ་ལ་ཆགས་གནས་འཇིག་སྟོང་གི་བསྐལ་པ་བཞི་དང་། བར་གྱི་བསྐལ་པ་དང་། བསྐལ་པ་ཆེན་པོ་དང་། ཡ་ཐོག་དང་མ་ཐོག་དང་། བར་ཁུག་དང་། ཡར་འཕེལ་བ་དང་། མར་འགྲིབ་པ་དང་། ཐ་མར་ནད་མཚོན་མུ་གེའི་བསྐལ་པ་དང་། མེ་ཆུ་རླུང་གིས་འཇིག་པའི་བསྐལ་པ་དང་། ཡང་རྫོགས་ལྡན་དང་། སུམ་ལྡན་དང་ཉིས་ལྡན་དང་། རྩོད་ལྡན་བཞི་དང་། བསྟན་པའི་དབང་དུ་བྱས་ཏེ་འབྲས་བུ་དང་། སྒྲུབ་པ་དང་། ལུང་དང་། རྟགས་ཙམ་འཛིན་པའི་དུས་སྡེ་བཞི་དང་གཞན་ཡང་སྟོན་པའི་བསྐལ་པ་དང་། སྒྲོན་མའི་བསྐལ་པ་ལ་སོགས་པ་དུས་ལ་བརྟེན་པའི་རྣམ་གྲངས་སྣ་ཚོགས་ཡོད་པ་ཤེས་པར་བྱའོ།

།ཉི་ཟླའི་བགྲོད་པ་ལ་བརྟེན་ནས་ཞག་གསུམ་གྱི་རྣམ་བཞག་བྱེད་དེ། ཉི་མས་རླུང་འགྲོས་ཀྱིས་གླིང་བཞི་འཁོར་བའི་ཡུན་ལ་ཆུ་ཚོད་དྲུག་ཅུ་ཐམ་པར་ངེས་པ་ཉིན་ཞག་གཅིག་དང་།

[7,12] The shortest [moment] earning that term is the completion of the act of merely snapping the fingers. The longest one, the time from when the Buddha first made the aspiration until he finally realized unexcelled enlightenment, can also be considered as one moment of completing an act.

[7,13] The duration of all things is labeled as time by the power of people's beliefs. It is therefore sometimes said that the present is simply what is present right now in its own time. All that happened previous to that is the past. What will occur later is the future. This is stated in terms of the [present] moment.

[7,14] Sometimes the present refers to the time this aeon was formed until it becomes void. What happened before that and what will happen later is considered past and future. It is permissible to mentally summarize the duration of time and give it such a name in terms of the labeled object.

[7,15] For this reason, based on our world there are the four aeons of creation, subsistence, destruction, and voidness. There are also the middle aeons, great aeons, descending [aeons] and ascending [aeons]; the undulating, increasing, and decreasing [aeons]. Finally there are the ages of sickness, warfare, and famine, as well as the ages of destruction by fire, water, and wind.

[7,16] There are moreover the ages of completeness, possessing three, possessing two, and of strife. In terms of the doctrine there are the four periods of fruition, of practice, of scriptures, and of adherence to mere signs. Furthermore, there is the aeon of darkness and the aeon of light and so forth. It should be understood that there are many such categories based on time.

[7,17] Based on the movements of the sun and moon, a system of three kinds of days is made.

[7,18] The duration it takes the sun, by the movement of the 'wind', to circumambulate the four continents is defined as sixty half-periods. This is called one solar day.

རང་འགྲོས་ཀྱི་དབང་གིས་ཟླ་བའི་ཆ་བཅོ་ལྔ་འཕེལ་འགྲིབ་རེའི་ཡུན་ལ་ཚེས་ཞག་ཅེས་བྱ་སྟེ། དེ་ལ་གནས་སྐབས་སུ་འཕེལ་འགྲིབ་རིང་ཐུང་ཡོད་ཀྱང་། དཀར་ནག་གི་ཕྱོགས་ཀྱི་མཐར་དོན་ལ་ཉིན་ཞག་གི་ཚད་ལས་ཅུང་ཐུང་བ་དང་། ཉི་མས་རང་འགྲོས་ཀྱིས་ཁྱིམ་རེ་རེ་འཁོར་བའི་ཡུན་སུམ་ཅུར་བཅད་པ་ལ་ཁྱིམ་ཞག་ཅེས་བྱ་སྟེ། ཉིན་ཞག་གི་ཚད་ལས་ཅུང་རིང་བའོ།

།ཞག་འདི་གསུམ་གྱི་དབང་གིས་ལོ་གཅིག་གི་དུས་རྣམས་བཞག་སྟེ། ཉིན་ཚེས་བསྡུན་ནས་ཚེས་ཀྱི་ཆད་ལྷག་དང་། ཚེས་ཞག་གི་དབང་དུ་བྱས་པའི་ཟླ་བ་རེ་དང་ཁྱིམ་ཞག་གི་དབང་དུ་བྱས་པའི་ཟླ་བ་གཉིས་རིང་ཐུང་མ་སྙོམས་པའི་དབང་གིས་ཟླ་བ་ཤོལ་འབྱུང་བ་སྟེ། ཉི་མ་ཁྱིམ་བཅུ་གཉིས་སུ་བགྲོད་པའི་དབང་གིས་གླིང་བཞིར་དུས་བཞི་འབྱུང་བ་དང་། ཟླ་བའི་ཆ་འཕེལ་འགྲིབ་ཀྱི་དབང་གིས་དཀར་ནག་གི་ཕྱོགས་དང་། གོ་ལའི་རླུང་འགྲོས་ཀྱིས་ཉི་མ་འཆར་ཚུལ་ལས་ཉིན་ཞག་འབྱུང་བའི་ཕྱིར། དེ་དག་ལེགས་པར་མ་བརྩིས་ན་མཐར་དཀར་ནག་གི་ཕྱོགས་དང་། དཔྱིད་སོགས་དུས་བཞི་ལོག་པར་འགྱུར་བའི་ཕྱིར། སྐར་རྩིས་ཀྱི་གཞུང་ལས་ཞིབ་པར་གཏན་ལ་ཕབ་པ་བཞིན་ནོ།

།དེ་ཡང་ལོ་གཅིག་ལ་ཟླ་བ་བཅུ་གཉིས་ཞག་སུམ་བརྒྱ་དྲུག་ཅུ། དེའི་སྔ་དྲོ་དང་ཕྱི་དྲོ་ཟན་ཟ་བའི་དུས་གཉིས་སུ་བརྩིས་པས་ཟ་མ་བདུན་བརྒྱ་ཉི་ཤུ་ཞེས་དང་ཡང་ཉིན་མོ་དང་མཚན་མོ།

ཉིན་གཅིག་ལ་ཡང་ཐོ་རངས་དང་སྔ་དྲོ་སོགས་སུ་ཕྱེ་བས། ཐུན་བཞི་དང་། དྲུག་དང་། བརྒྱད་དང་བཅུ་གཉིས་སུ་དབྱེ་བ་དང་།

ཟླ་བ་རེ་ལ་དཀར་ཕྱོགས་ནག་ཕྱོགས། ལོ་བཅིག་ལ་དབྱར་དགུན་སྟོན་དཔྱིད་བཞི་དང་། དགུན་སྟོད་དགུན་སྨད་སོགས་དུས་དྲུག་དང་། ལྷོ་བྱང་གི་བགྲོད་པ་གཉིས་ལ་སོགས་པའི་རྣམ་བཞག་བྱེད་དོ།

[7,19] In terms of the moon's own course, the duration of each of the fifteen parts of the moon for both the waxing and the waning periods is known as a lunar day. Although, for the moment, the waxing and waning are of [varying] lengths, at the end of the light and dark periods, [the lunar day] is in fact a little shorter than the length of a solar day.

[7,20] The duration it takes the sun, by its own movement, to circle through the zodiacs, each divided into thirty, is called one zodiacal day. It is slightly longer than the duration of a solar day.

[7,21] The time of one year is defined by means of these three kinds of days. Correlating the solar and lunar days, there are the omissions and extra [dates]. A double-month occurs because the months reckoned from lunar days and the months reckoned from zodiacal days are of an uneven length.

[7,22] The four seasons on the four continents occur because the sun travels through the twelve zodiacs. Due to the waxing and waning of the moon there are the light and dark periods.

[7,23] A solar day occurs from the way in which the sun rises because of the 'wind movement of the *gola*.' If these things are not calculated properly, the light and dark periods and the four seasons of spring and so forth will become mixed up. Time is therefore to be established minutely in accordance with the root texts of astrology.

[7,24] Moreover, one year has twelve months or three hundred and sixty days. By counting the times of partaking in early and late meals as two there are seven hundred and twenty meals and also [such a number of] days and nights.

[7,25] One day can also be classified, when dividing it into dawn, morning and so forth, into four, six, eight, or twelve periods.

[7,26] Each month has a light and a dark part. Each year has the four seasons of summer and winter, autumn and spring or six seasons such as the early and late winter and [spring, sowing time, mid-

།བགྲང་བྱ་ལོ་དང་བསྐལ་པ་ལ་སོགས་པ་དེ་དག་གཅིག་དང་བཅུ་དང་བརྒྱ་སོགས་བཅུ་འགྱུར་གྱིས་གྲངས་མེད་པའི་བར་དུ་བརྩིས་པའི་སྒོ་ནས་ཡུན་གྱི་ཚད་ཐམས་ཅད་གཞལ་ནུས་སོ།

།དེ་ལྟར་དུས་ཀྱི་རྣམ་བཞག་ལ་བརྟེན་ནས་སྔར་བསྐལ་པ་འདི་ཙམ་ན་སངས་རྒྱས་འདི་བྱོན་ནོ་ཞེས་དང་། མ་འོངས་པའི་དུས་དང་བསྐལ་པ་འདི་ཙམ་ན་འདི་འདྲ་འབྱུང་ངོ་ཞེས་དང་། ཐེག་པ་ཆེ་ཆུང་གི་ལམ་ལས་རང་འབྲས་དུས་ཅི་ཙམ་གྱིས་ཐོབ་པ། འགྲོ་བ་རྣམས་ཀྱི་ཚེ་ཚད་ཅི་ཙམ་ཡིན་པ་སོགས་ཤེས་པར་བྱེད་པ་ཡིན་ནོ།

།དངོས་པོ་རྣམས་དུས་སྐད་ཅིག་མའི་སྐྱེ་འགག་གི་ཕྲེང་བ་རིམ་བྱུང་ཙམ་ཡིན་པར་ཡང་རྟོགས་པར་འགྱུར་རོ།

།ཡང་ནང་སེམས་ཅན་གྱི་ཕུང་པོ་ལ་བརྟེན་ནས། སྐྱེ་བ་དང་། བྱིས་པ་དང་། གཞོན་ནུ་དང་། དར་བབས་དང་། ན་ཚོད་ཡོལ་བ་དང་། རྒས་པ་དང་། འཁོགས་པ་དང་། ཤི་བའི་དུས་སུ་བཞག་པ་དང་། ཕྱིའི་ཆོས་ལ། ས་བོན་དང་མྱུ་གུའི་དུས་སོགས་དང་། བྱ་བ་ལ་ལྟོས་ནས་དང་པོ་ཐུགས་བསྐྱེད་པ། བར་དུ་ཚོགས་བསགས་པ། ཐ་མར་སངས་རྒྱས་པ་ལྟ་བུ་སོགས་ཞེས་བྱའི་རྣམ་བཞག་ཐལ་མོ་ཆེ་དུས་ལ་བརྟེན་ནས་ཁོང་དུ་ཆུད་དགོས་པ་ཡིན་ལ། ད་ལྟ་ཇི་ལྟར་སྣང་བའི་དངོས་པོ་ལ་ད་ལྟའི་དུས་སུ་འདོགས་ཤིང་། དེ་ལ་བརྟེན་ནས་འདས་མ་འོངས་དུ་ཡང་སེམས་པར་བྱེད་དོ།

།དེ་ཡང་ད་ལྟའི་སྐབས་སུ་སེམས་ཅན་ཕལ་ཆེར་རྒས་པ། ཕལ་ཆེར་གཞོན་པ། ཕལ་ཆེར་སྐྱེ་བ་སོགས་མི་འདྲ་ཞིང་། རང་དུས་གང་ཡིན་ལ་ལྟོས་ནས་དེའི་སྔ་ལོགས་སུ་བྱུང་བ་རྣམས་འདས་པ། ཕྱི་ལོགས་སུ་འབྱུང་བ་རྣམས་མ་འོངས་པར་འཇོག་པ་ནི། རང་གི་སྣང་ཚུལ་ཙམ་ལས་དུས་སུ་བཏགས་པ་ཙམ་ཡིན་གྱིས་དོན་ལ་དུས་ཞེས་རྫས་སུ་གྲུབ་པ་གང་ཡང་མེད་པ

summer, and fall]. There is, moreover, the system of the two equinoxes.

[7,27] The numbers of years and aeons can be estimated in measures of duration by means of calculating with the numbers from ten and one hundred and, multiplying by ten, until the 'incalculable'.

[7,28] Based on this definition of time one can understand the statement "In the former aeon of such and such time, so and so buddha appeared!" "In such and such future time and aeon the buddha so and so will appear!" "The respective results through the paths of the greater and lesser vehicles are attained in such and such a time!" Also, "The life span of sentient beings is such and such" and so forth.

[7,29] One will also understand that all things are merely a successive occurrence as a chain of moments that arise and cease.

[7,30] Furthermore, based on the aggregates of sentient beings, the inner [phenomena], there are the descriptions of the periods of birth, childhood, youth, adolescence, middle age, old age, decrepitude, and death. Outer phenomena have the times of seed, sprout, and so forth. In terms of actions there are such as first aspiring, next gathering the accumulations, and finally attaining buddhahood. Understand that categories of knowable objects are for the most part to be comprehended based on time.

[7,31] The things appearing right now are labeled present time and based thereon one also comprehends the past and future.

[7,32] At present some beings are old, some are young and some are being born. There are various situations dependent upon whatever one's own time is. The past is what occurred earlier than that and the future is what will occur later on. This is merely labeling time according to how things appear to oneself, whereas so-called time has in fact no substantial existence whatsoever.

Just as there can appear various lengths of time during the dream-state, by the power of one's conceptualization some

རྨི་ལམ་ན་དུས་རིང་ཐུང་སྣ་ཚོགས་སྣང་བ་ལྟར་རང་གི་རྟོག་པའི་དབང་གིས་ཆོས་ཁ་ཅིག་འདས་པ། ཁ་ཅིག་ད་ལྟ་བ་དང་། ཁ་ཅིག་མ་འོངས་པར་བཞག་ནས་སྣང་གི། གནས་ལུགས་ལ་ཆོས་གང་ཡང་སྔར་འགགས་པ་མེད་ལ། ད་ལྟར་སྐྱེ་བ་འང་མེད། མ་འོངས་པ་ན་འབྱུང་བར་འགྱུར་བ་ཡང་མེད་དེ་དུས་གསུམ་མཉམ་པ་ཉིད་དུ་རྟོགས་ན་དུས་ལ་ཡང་དག་པར་མཁས་པ་ཞེས་བྱ་སྟེ་དེ་ལ་དགོངས་ནས་དུས་གསུམ་དང་། བསམ་གྱིས་མི་ཁྱབ་པའི་དུས་བསྟན་ཏེ་བཞིར་གསུངས་པ་ཡང་ཤེས་པར་འགྱུར་ལ། ཕྱོགས་རྣམས་ཀྱང་དུས་དེ་དང་འདྲ་བར་བརྟགས་པ་ཙམ་དུ་ཤེས་པར་འགྱུར་ཞིང་གནས་ལུགས་མཉམ་པ་ཉིད་ཁོང་དུ་ཆུད་པར་འགྱུར་རོ།

།དུས་ཀྱི་སྐབས་སོ།

phenomena are past, some present and some are defined as future and appear as being such. However, in reality, phenomena have no cessation in the past, no arising in the present, and no origination in the future.

[7,33] One is said to be perfectly learned in [the topic of] time when thus realizing the equality of the three times. Considering this, one will then understand four times by adding the inconceivable time to the three that have been taught. The directions will also be understood as mere imputations in that same way and one will realize the equality of the real condition.

[7,34] This was the chapter on time.

Notes

[1]. The ten topics (don bcu) are the seven chapters in *Gateway to Knowledge* Vol. I as well as the [four] truths, the [three] vehicles, and conditioned things and unconditioned things. The last three will appear in the coming volumes.

[2]. The Four Seals (phyag rgya bzhi) are: All composite things are impermanent. Everything defiling is suffering. All phenomena are empty and devoid of a self-entity. Nirvana is peace.

[3]. This line refers to the fourfold right discrimination of words, meanings, teachings and ready speech, also to be covered in future volumes.

[4]. Sun of Speech (smra ba'i nyi ma) is Manjushri who dispels the darkness of ignorance.

[5]. The perception of form by means of the mind placed in meditation is a very expansive way of perceiving, for example through using the concentration of repulsiveness or the divine sight acquired through meditation. The conceptual mind not placed in meditation is the normal and more limited way of perceiving by means of combining sound and object. (SG)

[6]. Words expressed by ordinary people are 'pillar,' 'jug,' etc. Words expressed by noble beings are, for example, 'the three gates of emancipation' or 'paramita.' (SG)

[7]. Earth, water, fire and wind.

[8]. A vow or an oath, such as taking ordination, is a 'form resulting from a taken promise.'

[9]. These seven types will be listed in Vol. II under disturbing emotions in the truth of origin.

[10]. These ten are the elements of the eye, ear, nose, tongue and body in addition to the elements of visible form, sound, odor, taste, and texture.

[11]. The elements of mind faculty, mind consciousness, and mental object.

[12]. They are called rhinoceros-like pratyekabuddhas because they live in solitude and attain enlightenment alone.

[13]. Although not desired, it will involuntarily result through the dependency of the unvirtuous action. (SG)

[14]. For instance, "A pot is impermanent because it is a product." (SG)

[15]. The nature of things here refers to the four truths and so forth. (SG)

[16]. Shechen Gyaltsab reiterates this: The difference between outsiders and insiders lies in whether or not the Three Jewels and the view of the Four Seals Signifying the Buddha's Words are accepted as being perfect objects of refuge and the perfect view. (SG)

[17]. The 62 views are taught in the *Sutra of Brahma's Net* as 18 based on the past and 44 on the future. The former are four types of proponents that everything is permanent, four types of nihilists, four types of claims that there is neither existence nor nonexistence, four types of claim that the divinity should not be abandoned, and two types of proponents of causelessness. The 44 latter are 16 types of claims that perception exists, eight types that it doesn't, eight claims that perception is neither absent nor present, seven types of nihilists, and five proponents of the view that nirvana is this life itself. Sometimes also 360 types of wrong views are mentioned. In the Five Tarka Groups, 'tarka' means logic, and they are: Samkhya, Vaibhasha, Mimanisaka, Digambara, and Charvaka. (SG)

[18]. 'Permanent' here means 'not resulting from causes and not arisen by means of conditions.' (SG)

[19]. Since even the nihilists claim that a self exists temporarily. (SG)

[20]. If it were the case that a permanent creator could perform the function of creating the world, then, because the cause is permanent all of the world would necessarily have to be created simultaneously without sequential order. This is evidently not so since we see the seasons gradually change. Moreover, since everything is appears in gradual sequence, a creator such as the Almighty is therefore not a permanent cause. (SG)

[21]. Since something devoid of causes for its being does not depend on any other thing, it must be either permanent or nonexistent. Crops should be able to ripen any time and so forth. This is because a thing would have to exist by virtue of itself independently of the gathering of causes and conditions. (SG)

[22]. It is established as being the nature of things that a flawless sprout will grow forth and continue to do so when and while its conditions for growing are present. (SG)

[23]. The term 'appearance' (snang ba) here means an instant of consciousness (rnam shes). (EPK)

[24]. Including the nose faculty, tongue faculty and body faculty. (SG)

[25]. The (SG) here says (yid bde) mental pleasure.

[26]. The sensations of pleasure, mental pleasure, pain and indifference. (SG)

[27]. All the defiling virtuous or unvirtuous deeds are in themselves not produced from karmic ripening, but will yield samsaric ripening as their individual results. (SG)

[28]. Eight faculties: life, mind, indifference and the five of faith and so forth. (SG)

[29]. This is because there are no other faculties of ripening present. (SG)

[30]. These nine aspects of liberation (rnam grol dgu pa) are also known as the ('dod nyon skor drug: chags pa, khong khro, nga rgyal, ma rig pa, log lta, tshul rtul mchog 'dzin, the tshom, phrag dog, ser sna). (Kenpo Konchok).

[31]. See [6, 26] for details of the nine.

[32]. Astrology (rtsi) also covers the system of reckoning dates and making calendars. (EPK)

[33]. When correlating that with the prevailing system of measuring time in the West, an Abhidharma 'moment' is 1.6 seconds; a 'minute' is 1.6 minute or 96 seconds; a 'period' which is 30 Abhidharma 'minutes' is 48 of our minutes. One 'breath' is four seconds; a 'water-measure' is 24 seconds; and a half-period is 24 of our minutes. (EPK)

Printed in the USA
CPSIA information can be obtained
at www.ICGtesting.com
JSHW012035140824
68134JS00033B/3062

9 789627 341291